SPEED-CUT QUILTS

SPEED-CUT QUILTS

DONNA POSTER

CHILTON BOOK COMPANY
Radnor, Pennsylvania

Designed by Anthony Jacobson
Manufactured in the United States of America

ISBN 0–8019–7889–0

Poster, Donna.
    Speed-cut quilts/Donna Poster.
        p.   cm.—(Creative machine arts series)
        Includes bibliographical references.
        ISBN 0-8019-7889-0
        1. Machine quilting—Patterns.   2. Patch-work—Patterns
    I. Title.   II. Series.
    TT835.P67   1989
    746.9'7—dc20   88-43312
                                                          CIP

    3 4 5 6 7 8 9 0   8 7 6 5 4 3 2 1 0

Credits
Graphics: Arn Poster, Sue Saiter, Donna Poster, Pamela Poole
Typing: Pat Oxley, Sue Saiter
Photography: John Anglin

To Arn, Zoë, and Laura
for their love, friendship
and
faith in me

CONTENTS

FOREWORD

Like many, I am full of grandiose plans but miniscule actions. I plan to make many full quilts—for Doris, for Mary, for this friend or that—but the reality is that I have only a few hours a week at night and on weekends to sew.

Reduced hours don't stop me from making quilts, though; making decisions does. Often I'm tired after a full day at work. If I'm in the middle of a project, I love to return to it and find the long hours rejuvenating. But if I have to exercise my brain to figure out a pattern, color, or yardage in order to start, I quit in exhaustion before I even begin.

That's the beauty of Donna Poster's book. Not only does she present 400 blocks in three sizes, but she's done all the hard work for us. She's figured out the yardage for each part of the block, as well as for lattice strips and borders.

You assemble all of the information you need for a quilt on an ingenious Play-Plan, step by step. Then you go to the fabric store knowing exactly how much you need of each fabric. With the Play-Plan, you don't even have to worry about colors until you reach the store.

Donna then shows you how to speed-cut many layers of fabric, using hard plastic templates called Speedies and a rotary cutter. By taping the plastic, you can cut intricate shapes, not just straight strips. This, too, is a tremendous time-saver.

With a Play-Plan, Speedies, a rotary cutter, and this book, you and I and our magic machines face a pleasant future full of speed-cut quilts.

Robbie Fanning

Series Editor, Creative Machine Arts

PREFACE

When I was a little girl, a neighbor had a baby after just one hour of labor. Many women in the community were incensed. "She has no right to say she had a baby. She has no idea what it's like!" they said.

The baby was beautiful, healthy and even durable.

I was puzzled by this attitude. If someday, through modern technology, I could produce a beautiful, healthy baby with one hour of labor, I'd be all for it—wouldn't you?

Today we have the tools to produce quilts in days, rather than months. These quilts are beautiful, they are healthy, and they are durable. I'm all for it. How about you?

This book is my way of helping you deliver such a quilt. Using speed-cutting tools and techniques, you can look forward to your own beautiful baby.

Donna Poster
Dallas, Texas

ACKNOWLEDGMENTS

Special thanks to:

Ellie Bird, Shirley Campbell, Jan Eufer, Janet Jelen, Teresa Kline, Paulette Murphy, Helen McCue Oelkrug, Tammy Peper, Carol Shaffer, Maria Simpson, Donna Benedetto, and Martha Neyland for their stitching, suggestions, and encouragement.

Robbie Fanning, for steering me through the mysterious world of publishing.

L. Harry Kershner, my father, for his teaching skills.

Alma S. Kershner, my mother, for her love of stitching.

Carrie Sitler, my grandmother, for her enthusiasm for quilting—and her warm lap.

Arn Poster, for his love, support and help. But most of all, for always being there when I need him.

INTRODUCTION

As I taught sampler quilt classes in my shop, I heard so often, "Well, I love my quilt but it's the last one I'll ever make." I thought, *How awful! I'm not creating quilters; I'm losing them.*

It was the cutting part everyone hated. I used to see this as a child when I watched the quilters try to coax someone else to cut for them. I saw it again in my classes, as my students became frustrated at the enormous amount of time involved before they could ever get to sewing. To be truthful, I hated the cutting part, too.

Then the rotary cutter was invented and the world of quilting came alive. We put away the sampler quilts and started turning out Rail Fences and Irish Chains, galore—any quilt design that used strips of fabric. They were gorgeous. Durable. Useable. We were delighted!

But sampler quilts are beautiful, too. People still asked for the class. I kept thinking, why couldn't we use the rotary cutter on the block pieces, too?

That's when the Speedies were invented. My husband, Arn, had already invented the Miterite, a plastic tool to use with rotary cutters. Now we put our heads together and came up with a series of plastic templates to help cut any block shape. By taping guidelines on the plastic, we could use the rotary cutter to make diamonds, triangles, rhomboids, and lots of other shapes. Now we could have stacks of precision-cut pieces in no time at all. We could make those beautiful block quilts in days without being limited to long strips.

We offered the sampler quilt class again, this time using Speedies, and the results were dramatically different. Now the students were doing the fun part right away. The cutting problems had disappeared.

But finding blocks was becoming a problem. Some were 12″ squares, others 14″, 16″,

The author, cutting out a new quilt.

10″, etc. Redrafting was not a big problem, but in the category of fun, it fell as low as cutting.

That's when I decided to write a book to make things simpler for my students—and you. The book would have 100 blocks, dozens brand-new. There would be four variations of each block, creating 400 different blocks. Each block would have templates for three sizes, a total of 1200 blocks. The templates would include seam allowances.

The book would have easy-to-read yardage guides plus a planning page and quilt layouts. It would guide the quilter from beginning to end.

1

This is my book. May you enjoy using it as much as I've enjoyed writing it. And may you make hundreds of speed-cut quilts.

A Word About Block Names: When I first started this book, I tried to be authentic in naming the "old" blocks. It became a time-consuming process. Since this book is meant as a tool and not a history, I've used the names as casually as they were probably used originally. I apologize to anyone I've offended with this off-handed approach to names.

Quilting is the sewing together of several layers of fabrics and batting. It is done for many reasons—warmth, body decoration, or simply our enjoyment of the process.

There are countless quilting techniques, materials, and tools. If ten quilters gather to do the same project, you will find ten different ways of doing it—and they will all be right. What works for one person will not work for another. Therefore, use whatever works best for you.

Obviously, I cannot put in this book every technique I've ever seen, heard, learned or used. It would create an encyclopedia and you'd be confused and overwhelmed. Fortunately, quilters are always on the lookout for a new technique, a new idea. They love to share these. Try them all.

What I can share in this book are the techniques and hints that I've found work best for the most people. But don't be afraid to try other techniques you hear about. That's what makes quilting fun and exciting.

If you prefer a spiral-bound book, as I do, most small job printers will do this for a reasonable fee. The pages have been designed to accommodate a spiral binding.

PART I

PLANNING YOUR QUILT

1

FOUR DECISIONS

Planning your quilt is often the hardest part of quilting, whether it is a gift for Aunt Hattie or a wall-hanging for your den. That's why I've written this book: to save you hours of planning and calculating. But you really only need to make four major decisions. If you will write each decision on a piece of scratch paper, you'll surprise yourself with a plan.

1. The Size: Which do you want to make?
   ☐ WALL HANGING: Decide where you want it and measure the space. The tablecloth sizes given below are usually just right.
   ☐ ALL-PURPOSE BLANKET: You'll want it long enough to tuck around your shoulders and under your feet. The twin size is great (approximately 72" x 102").
   ☐ LAP ROBE: Shorter than a blanket, but wide enough to tuck around the hips. The square tablecloth size is perfect (approximatcly 64" x 64").
   ☐ CHILD'S "PLAY BLANKET": Try the long tablecloth size—large enough to make a "tent," small enough to tote around (approximately 54" x 72").
   ☐ BEDSPREAD: Check the sizes given later in this book. They are long enough to cover your pillow with a generous tuck under it. They allow for a 14" to 16" drop over the side of the bed. When measuring, allow 2" to 4" extra for the "loft" of the quilt.
   ☐ TABLECLOTHS: Lightly padded quilts make beautiful tablecloths. I've included two standard sizes in this book: square 64" x 64"; oblong 54" x 72".
   ☐ SMALL PROJECTS: Have a few blocks left over? They are terrific for pillows, placemats, hot dishmats, tote bags, garment inserts— and more.

What's the best arrangement for these sampler blocks?

2. The Layout: Five Views
   Five views, A–E, are shown here. In Appendix B, I've given you five choices for the layout of your quilt, with the number of blocks and yardage you'll need. Which view you choose depends on your time, patience, and personal enjoyment. If you like to sit by the TV at night and hand quilt, choose a lattice layout, View C or E, and do lap-quilting. If

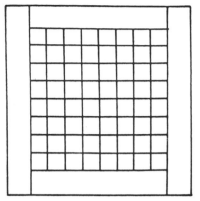

View A. Straight-set blocks

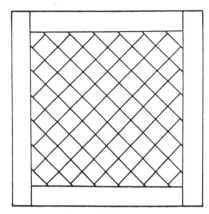

View B. On point

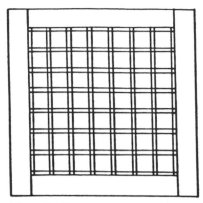

View C. Straight set with lattice

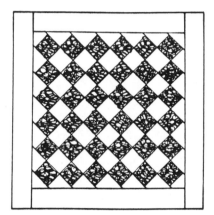

View D. On point, alternating blocks

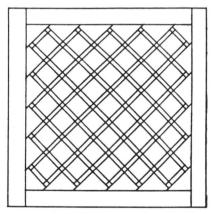

View E. On point with lattice

you need it done in a hurry, choose View D, On Point Alternating Blocks, (then half the blocks don't need to be pieced), sew the top, and then machine quilt it.

3. The Block: 400 Choices
Browse through the blocks in Appendix A. These are arranged by experience level: beginner, intermediate, advanced. Each block shows four ways to arrange the light, medium and dark colors.

You have two decisions to make about blocks: (1) which size? and (2) which block? For the first decision, size of the project, time, and your skill affect your decision. In the smaller projects, the 10″ blocks are generally better-looking, while in a large project, any size block looks good. If time is important, you'll have to make fewer blocks if you choose the 14″ size. As for your skill level, if

you're new to piecing blocks, keep it simple. If you're more advanced and enjoy piecing complex blocks, make a sampler using many different blocks. It's exciting to watch each new one come to life.

If time is short, your sewing skills are limited, and you're not crazy about the machine anyway, pick an easy block. Then repeat it, using great fabrics as your point of interest. You'll turn it out, assembly-style, in no time at all.

4. The Color
Color is so important to your quilt that I've devoted a special section to it (see Ch. 3). As a take-off point, though, you'll need to know where the quilt will be used. What are the colors used in that room? What are the person's favorite colors? If you can, be flexible about color. Rather than planning the color

completely before you start, choose fabrics at the store that you'll love to work with and shape the color from these. Then you'll really enjoy working on the quilt. At this point, all you need to decide is a general color scheme: rusts or navy and white or warm colors.

Putting It All Together

Now that you've made the four major decisions, you're ready to start. This is the scary part: What do I need? How much do I buy? How many pieces do I cut?

Relax! I've created a planning sheet to help you, called the Play-Plan. It will lead you, step-by-step, through the entire process. When you are done, it will all be on paper. Take this plan to your quilt shop to buy the fabric (they'll love you). Use it as a reference while cutting and sewing. Store it away and if you ever want to make this quilt again, the information will be right there. Remember to note the date you finished it, special events that happened while you were working on it, comments that will provide a jog to your memory and create a "quilt history."

Some people like to meticulously sketch out their quilts, while others like to cut, sew, and be totally surprised by the results. You may want to sketch out a quilt with one repeated block. As one block is connected to another, the placement of lights and darks creates incredibly different designs in the overall quilt. With just a little sketching time, you can be sure to have a pleasing effect.

You'll need only some graph paper and a pencil. Many quilters use colored pencils. I prefer seeing the dark to light shadings created with just a #2 lead pencil. If you're having trouble graphing the blocks, just trace them from the line drawing on the block page. Don't feel you have to draw *every* block. Only do enough to give you a picture of the pattern it creates.

A shortcut is to shade one block and photocopy it many times. Cut out the blocks and rearrange them until you like the overall pattern.

2

STEP-BY-STEP GUIDE TO THE PLAY-PLAN

All of your planning will be recorded on the Play-Plan. While the whole Play-Plan may look daunting to you, each part is entered in a logical, step-by-step order. When you are done, you not only have a plan of what to buy at the fabric store, but you will have a valuable record of what you've done.

To complete the Play-Plan, you will need tape or glue, scissors, a pencil, and either tracing paper or access to a photocopy machine. If you plan to do all your photocopying at one time, put paperclips on the pages you need to photocopy.

Start by photocopying both sides of the Play-Plan at the end of the book. Name the quilt you want to make and enter it—e.g., Mary's Quilt. On the back of the Play-Plan, enter today's date under **Date Started.**

Now follow me as I tell you what to do and show you a sample Play-Plan.

Step 1. Quilt Size

Choose a quilt size—crib, twin, double, queen, king, or tablecloth. You do not need to know the exact dimensions at this time, just the general size. Enter it on the Play-Plan. I chose an oblong tablecloth.

Step 2. Layout

Select a quilt layout from the five choices in Appendix B. Photocopy or trace your choice and save it for later. Enter the **View Number** and **Name** on the back of the Play-Plan.

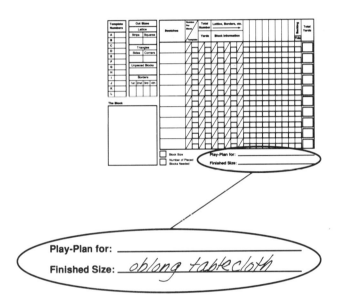

Play-Plan for: _____
Finished Size: _oblong tablecloth_

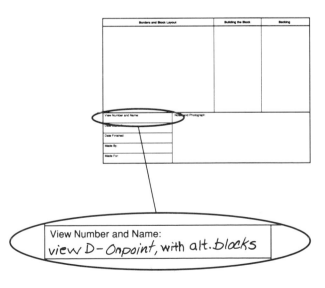

View Number and Name:
view D—Onpoint, with alt. blocks

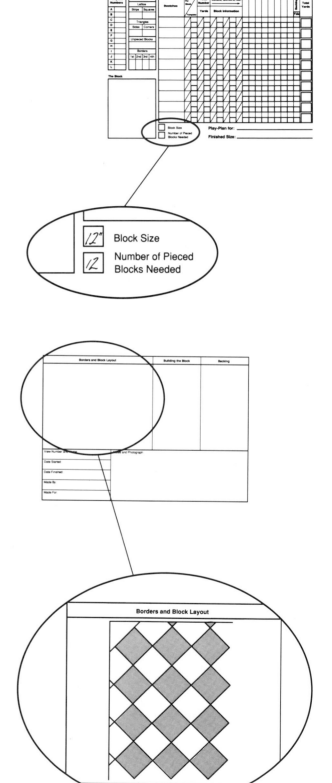

Step 3. Block Size

Choose a block size (10″, 12″, or 14″). Enter on the Play-Plan. Consult or photocopy Appendix B, Basic Information, across the page from the layout view you chose in Step 2. Enter the **Number of Pieced Blocks Needed.** (If you chose View D, ignore for now the number of unpieced blocks you need. We will take care of this later.)

Step 4. Block Arrangement

Look at the Quilt Layout you photocopied in Step 2. Circle the row of information for the quilt and block size you chose. Complete the size of the finished quilt you started in Step 1. Cut out the quilt layout you photocopied. Count the number of blocks across and down that you need. Cut off all extra blocks and the border and discard. Paste what's left on the back of your Play-Plan.

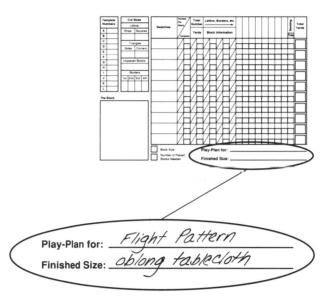

Step 5. Pattern

Choose a pattern from Appendix A. Photocopy the page. Circle the block you've chosen and the template numbers for the block size you've chosen. Write the name of the block on the Play-Plan above the finished size (see Step 1).

Play-Plan for: *Flight Pattern*

Finished Size: *oblong tablecloth*

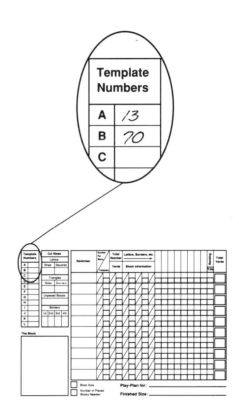

Step 6. Templates

On the Play-Plan, enter the template numbers you've circled.

The Block

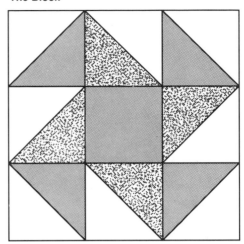

Step 7. Building the Block

On the photocopy from Step 5, cut out the block you've chosen, with the key to the fabric swatches next to the block. Save the rest of the page for later. Cut off the key to the swatches and save. Paste the block on the front of the Play-Plan. Paste the drawing that shows how the pieces go together on the back of the Play-Plan under **Building the Block.** Label the template letters.

Note: If you've chosen View A or B, you may want to photocopy the block as many times as you need blocks (Step 3), so you can see how the blocks look next to each other.

Building the Block

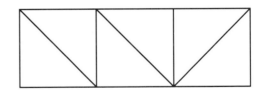

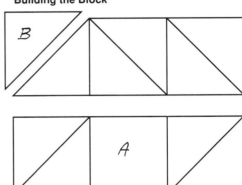

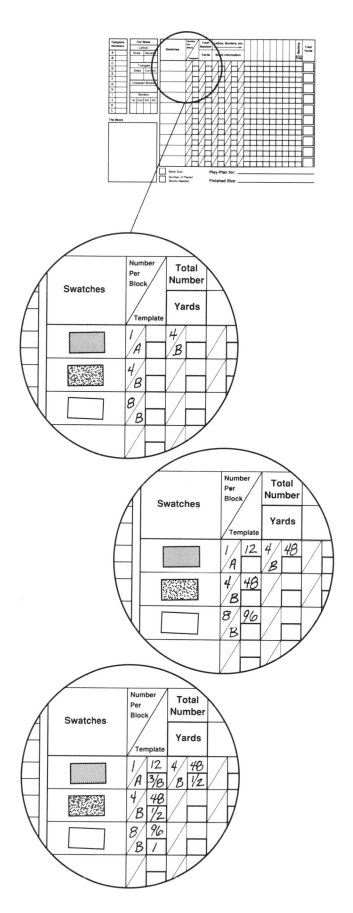

Step 8. Swatches

Cut apart the key to the swatches, making sure to leave the numbers and letters to the right of each swatch attached. Transfer to the Play-Plan the number of swatches per block and the template letter for each swatch. Then cut off the numbers and letters and paste in the swatches.

Step 9. Calculate Swatches

Calculate the total number of each swatch needed by multiplying the number per block times the total number of blocks needed (Step 3). For example, I need one of Template A for each of 12 blocks, so I need a total of 12.

Step 10. Block Yardage

Now calculate the yardage needed for each swatch by consulting Appendix C, Yardage Chart for Templates. Each template in each block has been given a number (Step 6). Look up the number of each template. You will see how many pieces of the template you can speed-cut from either ¼ yard, ½ yard, or 1 yard.

For example, I need 12 of Template A, #13. I can get 9 out of ¼ yard and 27 out of ½ yard. That means I can get 18 out of ³⁄₈ yard, so I write in that amount.

Match the amount of yardage needed for each swatch and write it on the Play-Plan.

Step 11. Border Width

The Quilt Layout you chose in Appendix B tells you what width of border you will have. Mine is 3″.

Oblong Tablecloth	10	3	4	8″	59 x 73
	12	3	4	3″	58 x 75
	14	2	3	8″	57 x 77

Look at Appendix D, Borders, for your width of border. It will tell you how wide each strip of your border is. Photocopy the appropriate page for your quilt.

Note: If stripes are used in any border strip, all the border strips in that quilt will have to be mitered. This requires extra fabric. Add twice the width of the border to the yardage requirements.

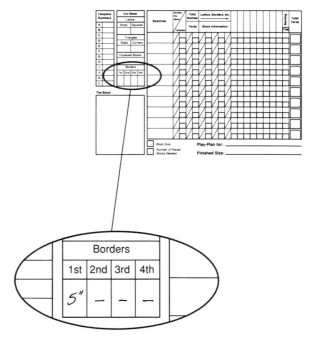

Step 12. Calculate Borders

Look at the chart in Appendix D. Find your border width and transfer the measurements for width of the border strips to the Play-Plan.

Swatches

1st border

Step 13. Border Color

Decide in what order you will use the swatches from Step 8 in the border. Generally, the small border next to the quilt body is dark and acts as a frame. Your nicest fabric is used for the outer border. Between these two, use whatever fabrics tie them together best. Write your decisions on the Play-Plan. I only have one border and I want it in my darkest color.

Step 14. Border Layout

Cut out the top and left side of the border you need from the photocopy you made in Step 11. Paste it on the back of the Play-Plan above and next to the Block Layout.

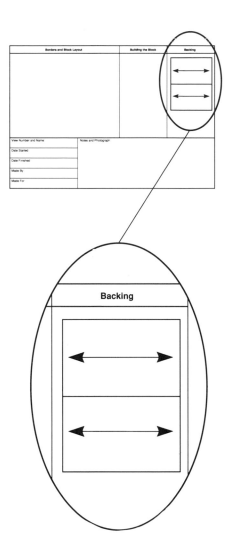

Step 15. Backing Piecing

Study Appendix E, Yardage and Piecing Guides for Backing. Photocopy or trace the piecing guide for the size quilt you are making. Paste it on the back of the Play-Plan.

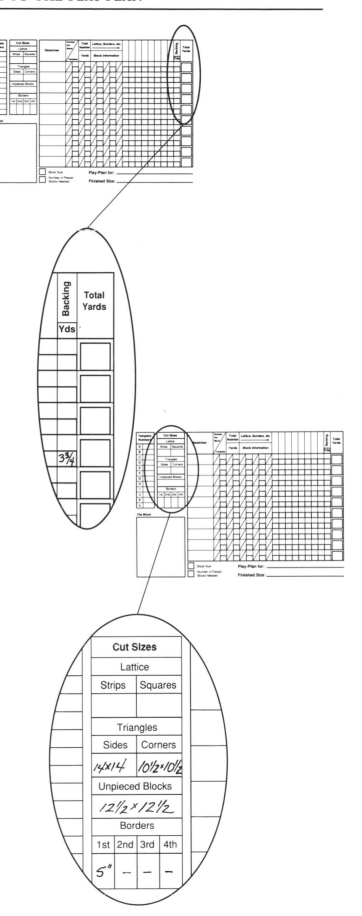

Step 16. Backing Yardage

Write the yardage you need for the backing on the front of the Play-Plan.

Note: If you want to construct your quilt block-by-block, quilting as you go, buy ¹/₃ more backing and one size larger batting (e.g., if making a queen size, buy a king-size batting).

Step 17. Sizes of Other Pieces

Look at the Cutting Notes on the Basic Information sheet you photocopied in Step 3. It contains the rest of the information you need to complete the Play-Plan. Each view has different requirements for lattices, triangles, and unpieced blocks. Transfer the cut sizes to the front of the Play-Plan.

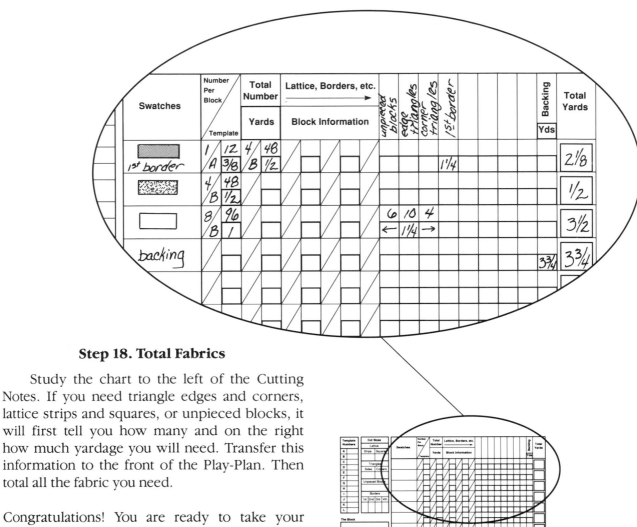

Swatches	Number Per Block / Template		Total Number — Yards		Lattice, Borders, etc. → / Block Information				unpieced blocks	edge triangles	corner triangles	1st border			Backing Yds	Total Yards
▓ 1st border	1 / A	12 / 3/8	4 / B	48 / 1/2								1¼				2⅛
░	4 / B	48 / 1/2														½
▭	8 / B	96 / 1							6	10	4					3½
										← 1¼ →						
backing															3¾	3¾

Step 18. Total Fabrics

Study the chart to the left of the Cutting Notes. If you need triangle edges and corners, lattice strips and squares, or unpieced blocks, it will first tell you how many and on the right how much yardage you will need. Transfer this information to the front of the Play-Plan. Then total all the fabric you need.

Congratulations! You are ready to take your Play-Plan to the fabric store and choose colors. You will also need batting. Make a note on the back of your Play-Plan about what kind and loft of batting you chose.

When you get home, paste a small rectangle of fabric in the appropriate swatches column.

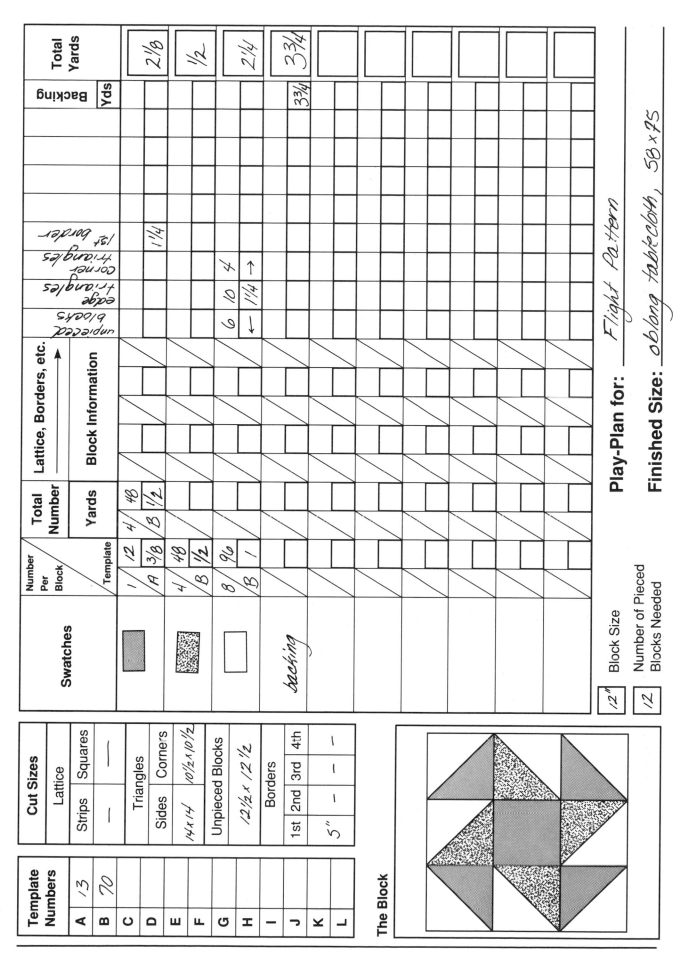

Play-Plan for: _Flight Pattern_

Finished Size: _oblong tablecloth, 58 × 75_

Template Numbers

A	13
B	70
C	
D	
E	
F	
G	
H	
I	
J	
K	
L	

Cut Sizes

Lattice	Strips	Squares
	—	—
Triangles	Sides	Corners
	14 × 14	10½ × 10½
Unpieced Blocks	12½ × 12½	
Borders	1st	5"
	2nd	—
	3rd	—
	4th	—

Block Size: 12"

Number of Pieced Blocks Needed: 12

The Block

Block / Yardage Chart

Swatches	Number Per Block / Template	Total Number / Yards	unpieced blocks	edge triangles	corner triangles	1st border	Backing (Yds)	Total Yards
(dark)	1 / A	12 / 3⁄8						2⅛
	4 / A	48 / ½						
(dotted)	4 / B	48 / ½				1¼		½
(white)	8 / B	96 / 1	6	10	4			2¼
			← 1¼ →				3¾	3¾
backing								

Backing

Building the Block

B

A

Borders and Block Layout

Notes and Photograph:

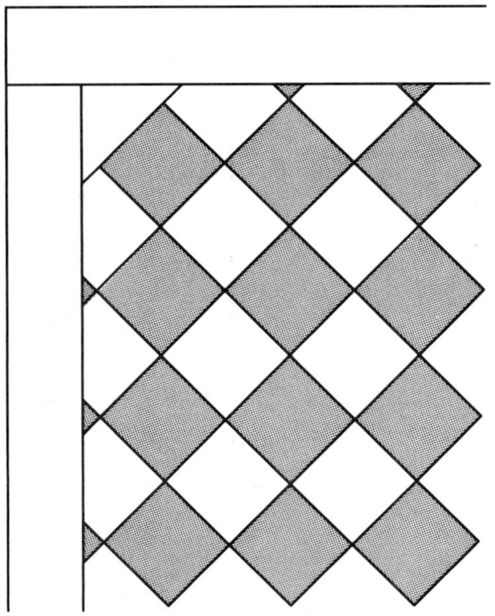

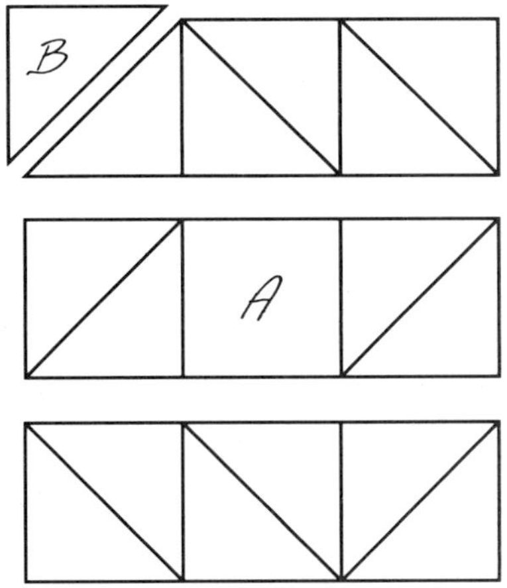

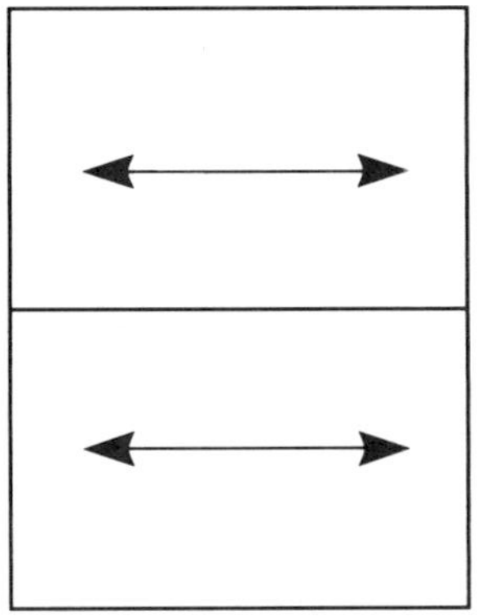

View Number and Name:

View D – Onpoint, with alt. blocks

Date Started:

Date Finished:

Made By:

Made For:

PART II

PREPARING TO MAKE YOUR QUILT

3

SCARED TO DEATH OF COLOR?

If you are truly afraid of color, nothing in my book or others will help. You need a teacher or store owner to guide your choices. That's the beauty of the Play-Plan. You know how much you need (the hard part). Let the expert help you choose the colors (the easy part).

Remember, too, that you don't have to reinvent the wheel. Look in quilt magazines, books, and calendars to find color schemes you like and borrow them.

If you're not sure you like the choices of the fabric store person, buy a small amount of each color and make one block. Then take it back to the store to be critiqued.

You can, however, teach yourself a great deal about color selection. With just a few guidelines to follow, color can be fun.

Color Family

First, pick one or two main colors and one or more accents. Be flexible, though—you may change your mind when you spot a piece of fabric you "have to have."

An easy way to start is to pick a fabric with the look you want. Study it. Are the colors bright and clear? Or grayed earth-tones? Whatever it is, keep all other colors in the family. A bright sailor blue added to a pile of teal, salmon, and taupe will screech like nails across a blackboard. But the same blue with a bright red and sunshine yellow will be terrific.

Look at the proportions of the colors—

Helen and Teresa
with their blocks planned.

which stand out? Which are small highlights? Is the print so tiny it's almost a solid? Is it a bold geometric? A frilly, fussy print?

Use the answers to these questions as a starting point.

When putting fabrics together to create a lovely quilt, there are as many different sets of rules as there are "experts." The soft, subtle quilt that warms Sue's heart is simply dull and bland to Nancy. And the bold, vibrating colors Nancy enjoys are garish to Sue.

Here are a few observations I've made along the way.

Color Values

Value is the lightness and darkness of the fabrics. The contrasts and shadings created by the values you choose will determine the character of your quilt.

As you look through the pages of block designs, note the light, medium, and dark values and what they do to the block. In general, for a *strong,* bold look, use high contrast colors; a very light next to a very dark (your quilt will take on the color of the dark fabric).

For a *subdued,* quiet look, use low contrast colors. To create a dark, but quiet quilt use darks and mediums, but no lights. For a light, but quiet, look use lights, mediums, and no darks.

In a way, there are no mediums. If you put a medium fabric next to a light, there will be a *contrast.* If you want to soften this contrast, insert fabrics that "shade" the two together.

If you like the look of a particular block, it can best be achieved by following the values shown in the sketch. Do feel free to change them, though. Experimenting is fun.

Prints and Stripes

The general rule is to use a wide variety of print sizes and styles, including an occasional solid. This is the surest way to achieve an interesting quilt.

For a dramatic, bold look, use all solids. Magnificent quilts are made with a repetition of one or two blocks using just two high-contrast solids.

Soft prints and low contrast will produce a lovely subdued, mellow quilt. (Yes, Virginia, you can use lots of tiny prints together.)

Cut up large prints at random for an exciting sense of movement. The pieces will not be exactly alike, yet will definitely feel like parts of a whole. Don't be afraid of ending up with headless pheasants and finless fish—you're sure to like the results of experimenting this way.

If you have many different points of interest in the design, as in a sampler quilt, keep the number of colors and prints to a minimum. If, however, you are repeating a few simple pieces or blocks, interest can be added with many prints and colors.

Don't bother about tiny bits of odd color in a fabric. If you're making a maroon and blue quilt and that perfect navy has tiny bits of rust in the print, use it. When the quilt is done, your eye will change that rust to maroon.

Some prints create illusions of stripes when viewed from a distance. These usually require no special cutting for small pieces. But for borders and lattice strips, it is important to have the stripe effect line up with the long edge. To achieve this, simply cut these long edges parallel to the selvage and the design will fall right into place.

You may, at times, find a design with areas or motifs you would like to highlight. These will have to be cut individually. (Be sure to buy extra fabric to account for the waste). Be aware of the top and bottom of this motif in relation to your finished quilt. (The transparent Speedies are perfect for centering these special prints).

Play with stripes—you can create terrific effects with them. I've included them in many of the blocks. Just be sure you buy enough fabric (see the note in Step 11 of Chapter 2).

Stay Flexible

When you're making a quilt, things happen along the way: you need more of a certain fabric and it's no longer available; the test was wrong and it turned out to be a boy; Aunt Ruth wants a purple quilt and you hate purple. The list is endless.

Relax—let's consider some alternatives. That fabric you need—could you substitute something close to it? Use a coordinating rather than a matching fabric in the border? Make a lap throw, pillow or tote bag of this piece and start over on another quilt?

That boy baby—you can give a blue quilt to a baby girl but people are funny about pink for boys. Put it away for the next girl. Now take the quickest block in the book, do an "on point, alternating blocks," and whip a new one up fast.

You can't picture yourself sewing a whole purple quilt? Try to convince Aunt Ruth that a tiny accent of purple would be much more dramatic than a whole quilt of purple. If you can't get out of it, plan a *fast* quilt. After all, this should be enjoyable to you, too.

If you're into one of those projects where it's *all* gone wrong and you just hate it, fold it up neatly, put it in a box, and hide it on the top shelf of a backroom closet. Then forget about it and start something else. A small project that's a guaranteed success will get you quilting again. Someday you'll find that box and you'll probably find it works this time. If it *still* doesn't, give it away.

Developing Color Schemes You'll Love

Select prints because they look good together. The overall design of a fabric will change drastically when cut up in small pieces. A fabric that is ugly on the bolt may be just the thing needed to make your quilt gorgeous.

Black can add excitement (what a shame that we associate it with funerals and villains' hats). Use it to set off brilliant splashes of color. They'll positively vibrate.

Be a little daring if you can. Try an accent of an odd color for a really striking look. Tuck a touch of lavender in a blue quilt. Or a bit of teal in a beige piece.

Don't try to coordinate everything. Study nature and you'll see all sorts of colors together. Part of the beauty of a forest is the many shades of green in the different trees, mixed with the highlights of sun and shadows. A beautiful sunset will include yellow, magenta, brilliant blues, purple, and white. What a magnificent quilt that would make!

After selecting your fabrics, walk away, turn and take a fast look. Did any stand out? If so, use this either as your main color or in small amounts as a highlight. Do any blend together? Then they'll perform as one fabric and you'll lose the effectiveness of both. Did your fabrics please you? Then, **go for it.**

And don't ignore your backing fabric. A really smashing print will make your quilt interesting and reversible. If you choose a large print, buy an extra repeat per seam so the design can easily be matched. Rely on your own intuition. It helps to have someone play with the fabrics with you, but for a final choice, you are the one who knows best what *you* like.

Try not to get a set picture of what your quilt will look like. It's virtually impossible to visualize it as it really will be. Pick fabrics that work well together; then enjoy watching your quilt come to life.

4

PURCHASING THE FABRIC

Now that you've decided on size, layout and block, and have made a Play-Plan, it's time to buy fabric. Take your Play-Plan to the store.

Double-Checking Yardage

Your Play-Plan tells you how much you need of each fabric, but you may need more if you decide to quilt your blocks one at a time. *For block-by-block method,* purchase ¹/₃ more backing fabric, and one size larger batting piece (e.g., if making a queen size, purchase a king-size bolt).

Buying Fabric

100% cotton is the sturdiest, most durable fabric for quilts. It also has a slight nap, which helps keep the pieces together while stitching.

Buy enough. Fabrics can disappear from a store overnight and never be available again. Many a quilter has become frustrated and discouraged when she finds that the piece she's run out of is no longer available. Better to have extra—you can make marvelous quilts with scraps.

For this same reason, if you see a fabric you really like, buy it. Manufacturers often produce only one run of a fabric. You may never find it again. How much to buy? My rule of thumb is: (1) if I'm absolutely wild about it, I'll buy at least 2¹/₂ yards (enough for an unpieced border); (2) if

Ellie, Jan, and Janet selecting their fabrics.

it's a really super background fabric, I'll buy 5 or 6 yards; and (3) if it's a nice accent piece, but a "little goes a long way," I'll get 1 to 2 yards.

Remember, if you use stripes in your blocks, you'll need ¼ to ⅓ more fabric.

Store fabric neatly, preferably in boxes and according to color. Avoid airtight plastic bags, which will eventually cause your fabric to deteriorate.

Preparing Fabric for Quilting

Prewashing is recommended to preshrink the fabric and remove excess sizing. The grain is then reliable just as it comes from the dryer. It has the extra advantage of washing out any excess dye from the darker fabrics, and you'll have a washable quilt when finished.

Snip a little ¼″ triangle off each of the four corners of your fabric before tossing it in the washing machine. This cuts down on ravelling and tangling. Wash lights and darks separately.

Try a light spray of fabric sizing when ironing—it's much easier to get the wrinkles out. It also adds a bit more body, making those small pieces easier to work with. If you're working with a lot of bias cuts, this is a "must."

After laundering, trim all selvages off before cutting.

A SUPPLY CHECKLIST

☐ **Rotary cutter:** large, industrial size.

☐ **Cutting mat:** should be at least 18″ × 24″. Larger (i.e., 24″ × 48″) is even better if storage space is no problem. It's nice to have one with grid markings.

☐ **Cutting ruler:** this must be thick enough to use with the rotary cutter. Although you can use whatever you want, we recommend the Miterite, as it is transparent and is 8″ × 24″ with ⅛″ markings and a 45° angle on one end. *It is important to use the same ruler throughout a project.*

☐ **Speedy cutting templates:** make your own cardboard templates from the full-size templates in Appendix F, or buy Speedies (available at your local quilt store or from Holiday Designs). The Speedies used in this book are

    Square/Rectangle

    Triangles

    45° Diamond/Parallelogram

Not necessary, but nice to have, are a Miterite, Jr., and small square (6½″). Make your own from quilter's template plastic or oaktag, but this will slow you down because you can't use a rotary cutter with these materials.

☐ **Dressmaker pins:** for piecing.

☐ **Long, large-headed quilting pins:** you won't know how you lived without them.

☐ **Artist's (drafting) tape or quilter's tape:** Artist's (or drafting) tape works best, as it will not leave a residue; available at any art supply store. Any width from ¼″ to 1″.

☐ **Safety pins:** nickel-plated, 1″ long, about 350 will baste a double-bed-sized quilt.

☐ **Walking foot or even-feed foot:** use this for machine quilting. It will feed the three thicknesses of your quilt evenly.

☐ **Common sewing tools:** scissors, seam ripper, thimble, etc. No list here, as everyone has her favorites.

A modern-day quilting bee!

☐ **Fabric sizing spray:** needed only if you prewash your fabrics. Especially helpful when you're working with a lot of bias seams.

☐ **Marking pen (water soluble):** needed to make quilting lines. If all your quilting stitches follow seam lines, you won't need a marker.

☐ **Quilting needles:** (for hand quilting only), use "betweens," size 8 to 10. The smaller the needle, the shorter the stitch.

☐ **Lap frame:** only for hand quilting block-by-block.

☐ **Hoop or floor frame:** only for hand quilting whole quilts.

☐ **Pearl cotton #3:** only for tying quilts; has sheen, is washable, easy to handle. Use two or three strands.

☐ **Batting:** look for the word "Bonded." It holds up well in the washing machine and needs very little quilting. Use lighter weights for clothing and table coverings, medium to heavy for quilts.

☐ **Flannel or fleece:** often used as batting for clothing or table coverings.

☐ **Sewing thread:**
   ☐ My favorite is a large cone of natural-colored thread. I wind a dozen bobbins with it and I'm set for hours. You may use odds and ends of good quality thread for piecing, as it does not have to match the fabric.

   ☐ To match backing fabric (for machine-quilting only).
   ☐ To match outer border (which becomes the binding).
☐ **Invisible thread:** for machine quilting only.
☐ **Quilting thread:** for hand-quilting only.

6

SPEED-CUTTING

Today's tools enable us to accomplish in hours or even minutes a job which used to stretch into long, tedious days. Instead of tracing laboriously around a template and then cutting out one shape, we stack up many layers of fabric and cut them all with a rotary cutter.

By putting quilting or artist's tape on your plastic template (the Speedy) to guide your cuts, you can cut any shape. Here's how.

Taping Your Speedy

You can create a precision-cutting template with masking tape.

1. Choose Speedy or Miterite to fit shape of design to be cut. Pattern *must* include seam allowances.

2. Place speedy on pattern, lining up two outer edges of tool with pattern. Tape all other pattern sides on tool with masking tape. Place tape *around* the pattern, *not inside* it. When laying tape down, lean over the table, so you are looking straight down on the pattern.

3. Instructions will refer to the "free edge" and the "taped edge" of your template. *All cuts are made on the free edges.*

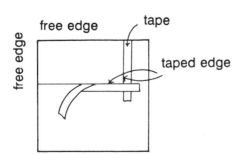

Janet and Jan, speed-cutting.

Cutting with Speedies

1. Always start by cutting a straight edge on your fabric.

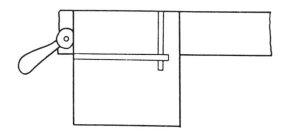

2. Place a taped edge on this cut edge of fabric. Cut along free edge.

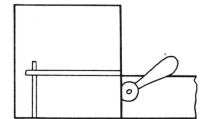

3. Rotate Speedy: position taped edges on these two cuts. Cut along both free edges.

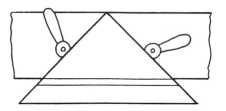

4. Triangles may be cut 2 ways: with straight grain on long edge; or straight grain on short edges.

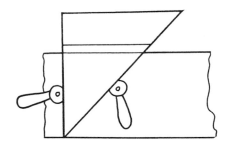

Cutting Multiples

1. Measure width of taped piece. Stack up to 12 layers of fabric. Using a new blade, cut many strips of that width.

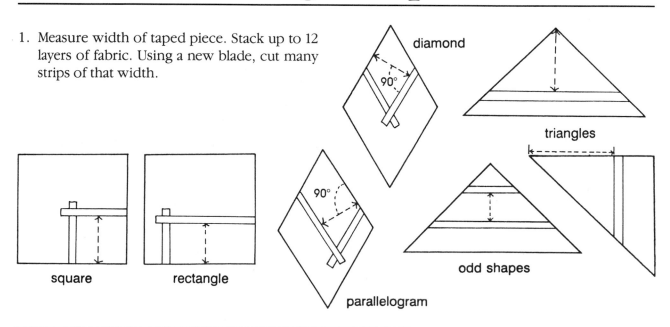

square

rectangle

diamond

90°

parallelogram

90°

triangles

odd shapes

2. Move template along this strip, cutting free edges.

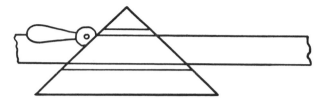
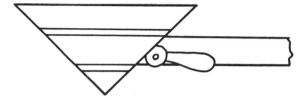

Double Cuts

A "double-cut" is a pattern piece requiring a combination of Speedies/Miterite to tape and cut.

Measure and cut *all* double-cuts in the same manner as "multiple pieces." At times, it may be necessary to flip a template instead of rotating it. Examples of common double-cuts are illustrated.

for this shape: **tape this way:**

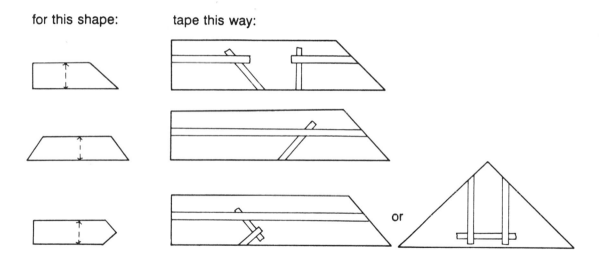

Traditional Cutting

If you don't have a Speedy, you'll have to use the traditional way to mark and cut. (The rotary cutter cannot be used with lightweight plastic or oak tag.)

1. Trace pattern pieces on a sheet of sturdy template plastic or oak tag. Use a ruler: accuracy is important.

2. Cut template pieces out.

3. On wrong side of fabric, with wrong side of template up, trace around each template as often as needed. Use a sharply pointed #2 pencil or, for dark fabrics, use a white or silver pencil. Slant the pencil point "into" the template to get the line as close as possible.

4. Cut out each piece with scissors.

7

MACHINE PIECING

A balanced tension is important. Your stitching should not draw up the fabric (if it does, your tension is too tight or your stitches too long.) You should not see the thread from the other side.

For piecing, use a medium to small stitch (12–15 stitches per inch). Since there is no back-stitching at the ends of most of the seams, these small stitches will not pull out.

Use a fine to medium machine needle size 10 (70) to 12 (80). Change the needle often; it will make a difference in the quality of your stitching.

Poke through your box of machine accessories and find the single-hole needle plate to replace that wide-hole (zigzag) plate. You'll have better control of your fabric. Don't set your machine on zigzag. If you don't have a single-hole needle plate, decenter the needle to the left or right—but remember that it changes the width of your seam allowance.

Ellie, stitching the last border.

Easing

Don't be alarmed if, occasionally, you need to ease two pieces together. Just pin or hold the two ends in place and *gently* pull the fabric as it is sewn. If possible, sew with the larger piece against the feed dogs. (If the two pieces simply don't fit, check to make sure you've cut them from the correct templates.)

Note: If sewing bias to bias, never pull to ease. "Pat" them in place.

The ¼" Seam

Finding and maintaining a perfect ¼" seam will make your piecing time enjoyable. Pieces fit together; ripping is almost nonexistent. To find a reference point on your sewing machine, mark a line ¼" from the edge of a piece of paper. Insert the machine needle into the line. Drop the presser foot. Find an easy *sighting* at the edge of the paper (the edge of the foot, the presser foot opening, etc.). You may want to use masking tape or a seam guide. On some machines, you can decenter the needle so that the needle falls ¼" away from the sighting you choose. Learn to guide the cut edge of your fabric along this sighting and you won't have to spend time marking your seams.

About that ¼" seam—make it a *scant* ¼".

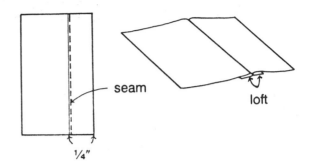

There's a bit of loft in the fabric at any seam, creating a shortage in the size of that piece. It may seem insignificant, but a block with eight pieced seams can end up much shorter than a block with only two seams. Using scant ¼" seams allows for this loft.

To Pin or Not to Pin

There are people who would refuse to sew if they had to pin. Others create metal sculptures of their seams. The majority of us use pins only at key places.

In general, a few well-placed pins help on any bias seam, set-in blocks, eight-point stars, long seams, and matched seams.

Pin across seams, but always remove a pin before you come to it. Sewing across pins is

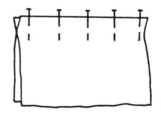

hard on your needle, weakens the seam, and shifts the fabric at that point.

Matching Seams

1. Always press matching seams in opposite directions.

2. For perfect matching, pin seams together *at* the seam line. Stitch up to the pin before removing.

3. With practice, most seams can be matched

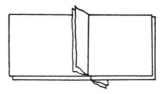

quite nicely by butting them together with your fingers and holding them as close as possible while stitching.

Set-In Pieces

1. Sew each side of the set-in piece as two separate seams.

2. Stitch each seam *away from* the inside corner.

3. The first seam is sewn with the set-in piece on the bottom. The last stitch should meet the end stitch of the adjoining seam. Backstitch two or three stitches.

4. The second seam is sewn with the set-in piece on top. The last stitch should meet the end stitch of the first seam. Backstitch two or three stitches.

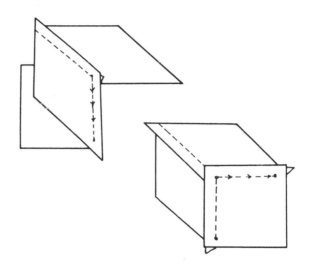

Joining Eight Points

1. Sew four sets of two pieces each.

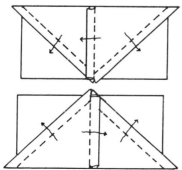

2. Press and join as shown. If sewing bias pieces (as in eight-point stars), be *very* careful *not* to stretch the seams or edges.

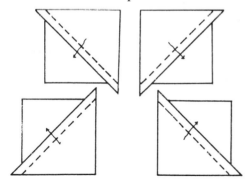

3. Join and press these units as shown. Trim extending corners at joining points.

4. Insert pin straight through both pieces, at point where all seams meet. Holding this pin straight out, pin ⅛" on either side of center point, as illustrated. Remove center pin.

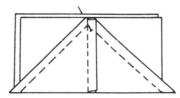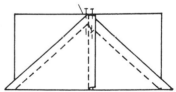

5. Starting about 2" before the center point, stitch a ¼" seam to about 2" past the center point. Be careful not to stretch the fabric. Sew *over* the pins slowly, gently pushing heavy thicknesses under the machine foot. (Yes, I know I said don't sew over pins, but this is an exception.)

6. Stitch entire seam, sewing *on* the 4″ center seam.

7. Press seam to one side. If center does not lie flat, restitch center, making a slightly larger seam at the center point.

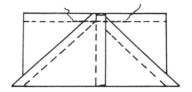

Pressing

1. Never press seams open; always press to one side. Whenever possible, press the seams toward the darker fabric. Exception: when one seam will be matched to another, press them in opposite directions.

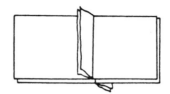

2. Press with or without steam, as you prefer. Steam can change the shape and size of a piece, so use it with caution.

3. Press *gently.* You are not ironing a pair of

blue jeans.

4. Press on the right side, moving the iron in the same direction you're pressing the seam.

Angles and Points

You'll find that, after awhile, you've become quite good at judging ¼″ areas. But until then, you may want to mark a few corners with ¼″ seams (remember, *scant*). These are the most difficult to judge:

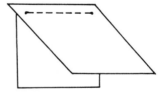

1. Sewing two different angles together.

2. Sewing any seam which *must* end ¼″ from the edge, as for set-ins.

3. Matching two angled seams.

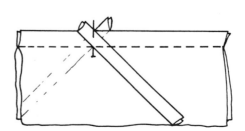

"Factory" Method

When sewing several identical units, feed them through the machine without separating them. It is faster and easier to keep your pieces in order. Later you can clip them apart.

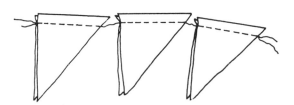

Handling Bias

Next to maintaining a ¼″ seam, handling bias is the biggest (and most ignored) secret to easy piecing.

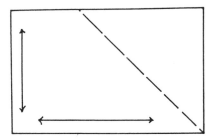

1. Learn what bias is and form the habit of being *aware* of it: *straight grain* is the two directions (lengthwise and horizontal) of the threads used to weave the fabric); *bias* is any other direction; *true bias* is a 45° angle to the straight grain.

2. When sewing a bias edge to a straight edge, try to sew with the bias piece on the bottom. If it's on top, your machine foot will stretch it by pushing the fabric ahead.

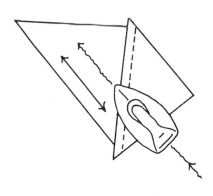

3. When pressing a piece with a bias edge, either set the iron down and pick it up without moving it or gently move the iron *with the grain* of the bias piece.

4. If you've pre-washed a fabric that will be cut up into triangles, diamonds, or other bias shapes, use a spray-on fabric sizing when ironing it.

5. As your project grows in size and weight, learn to handle it flat or folded, rather than picking it up at a raw edge. The weight will stretch any unstitched bias edges.

Blocking

When all of your blocks are done, you will probably find they are slightly different sizes. If any are just a bit oversized, the edges can be trimmed off. If any are a little too small, a steam iron may be used to block them a bit bigger.

If, however, any are much too big, or too small (1/2" or more), you'll need to rip a seam or two and restitch. Don't worry—it happens to all quilters.

Now decide whether you want to construct the whole quilt with borders and quilt it (Chapter 8) or quilt each block as you go (Chapter 9).

8

FINISHING THE WHOLE QUILT

Consult your Play-Plan and sew the blocks together according to the layout you chose. When constructing on-point quilts, triangles at edges will hang off. When attaching next row, sew across this overhang. Trim overhang to ¼″ seam. This method gives the squares a floating illusion.

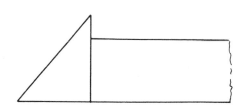

Borders

First Border only: Lay entire pieced center on a flat surface. Pin one piece of border fabric to side edge, right sides together. Cut second side piece the same length. Pin to second side edge. If piece is too long, trim both pieces and ease the first side. Stitch. Attach end pieces in same manner.

Remaining borders should not require measuring and pinning, but are otherwise added in the same sequence.

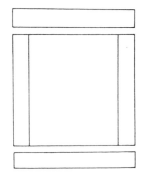

Hand-quilting on a frame.

41

Mitering Borders—Speedy Method

1. Sew border strips to sides. Backstitch at beginning and end of each seam. Leave seam allowance at ends free. Place short edge of Miterite against seam line, as shown. Draw along angled edge (seam line).

drawing the seam line

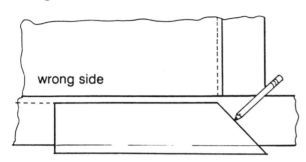

2. Move seamline guide of Miterite over line drawn in Step 1. Draw along angled edge as shown. Repeat on all corners. Sew, right sides together, on seam lines. Trim along cutting line.

drawing the cutting line

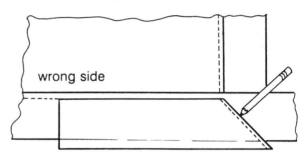

Mitering Borders—Traditional Method

1. Sew borders to quilt, centering each strip on the quilt edge. Border strips should extend equal amounts on both ends. Stitching must stop 1/4" from each end. Backstitch to secure.

2. With wrong side up, gently smooth the left border over the right one. Draw a diagonal line from the inner seam to the point where outer edges cross.

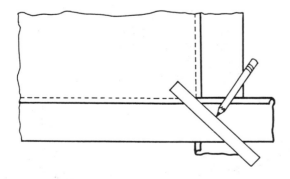

3. Fold quilt, right sides together, till adjacent border edges are lined up with each other. Stitch along diagonal line, stitching from outer edge to inner seam. Do not catch original border seams. Backstitch.

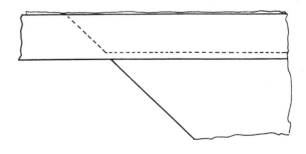

4. Check corner shape—should form a 90° corner. Trim seams to 1/2". Press open.

Basting the Quilt

You'll need a large, flat surface to work on. Mark the center of this surface and the center of your quilt backing. Matching these centers, lay the quilt backing, *wrong side up,* on the table. Center the batting on top of the backing. Center the quilt top, right side up, on the batting.

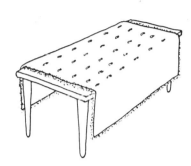

To be sure there are no folds or wrinkles on the bottom, pull gently on each of the four sides of the backing fabric. Repeat this every time you reposition the quilt during the basting process.

Starting at the center and working out, pin through all layers, using 1"-long, nickel-plated safety pins. Position pins every 3"–4". Avoid placing any directly on a line to be quilted.

When entire area on top of the table has been basted, carefully slide the quilt so an unbasted area is now on top. Repeat until quilt is completely basted.

Check the underside for pleats and wrinkles. You may want to rebaste an area.

Hints for Machine Quilting

Machine quilting is possible today because of the walking foot (or even-feed foot) and transparent thread.

1. When quilting over two or more colors of fabric, use a clear thread on the top. You'll need to loosen the top tension to get a perfect stitch. For the bobbin, choose a good sewing thread to match the backing fabric.

2. With a walking foot, you will not have to push or pull the quilt through the machine. Be careful, however, that the weight of the quilt does not create a drag.

3. Where to quilt is personal. Most people pick out specific seam lines and follow them. This is easy when only quilting blocks. Your movement is limited, though, when machine quilting a large item. You'll need to choose your quilting lines with this in mind. There are attachments available to allow a free movement of the fabric while stitching. You may want to experiment with these. (See the Bibliography for a good book on machine quilting.)

4. For machine quilting, use a longer stitch—6 to 8 stitches per inch—it feeds through easier and has a puffier look. If you're using a clear thread on top, loosen your upper tension to prevent the thread from breaking.

The trick to quilting the full top is to learn how to handle bulk. Roll each side tightly toward the center quilting line. A few pins help keep these two rolls in place.

Fold as shown to make a manageable bundle to put in your lap.

Using a walking foot and a long machine stitch, sew the entire length of this quilting line.

Reroll the quilt to the next area and stitch.

Repeat till quilt is done.

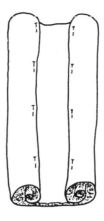
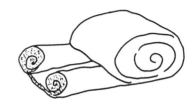

9

FINISHING THE QUILT BLOCK-BY-BLOCK

If you decided to use the block-by-block method to quilt, cut the following, depending on the size of your block.

Blocks	Cut Backing	Cut Batting
10"	15x15	14x14
12"	17x17	16x16
14"	20x20	19x19

For borders, cut four pieces of batting the width of your finished border, plus 3" (for example, for a border totaling 7" in width, cut batting 10" wide).

Cut two of these long enough to fit the sides of your finished quilt center. (When measuring, hold quilt edge taut or your borders will be too short). Cut remaining two long enough to fit the ends *after* the side pieces have been sewn on.

Cut four pieces of backing fabric the same way as the batting pieces.

Machine Method

Note: This method is recommended for "blocks with lattice" only.

1. Center pieced block on batting and backing. Pin baste.

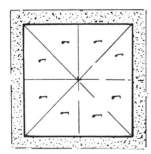

2. Machine quilt as desired.

3. Add lattice strips. Place first strip on block, right sides together. Stitch ¼" seam through *all* layers, including batting and backing.

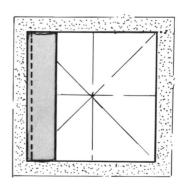

4. Sew second strip on opposite edge.

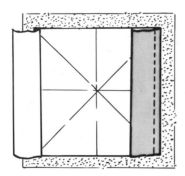

5. Sew second block to second lattice strip. Sew third lattice strip to second block.

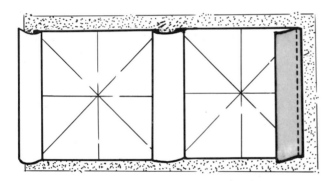

6. Repeat until all rows are completed.

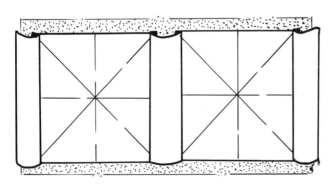

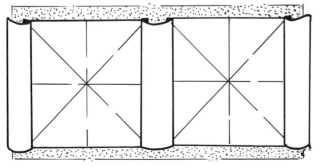

7. On back side: trim batting so one side *overlaps* the other ¼". Then pull batting back so edges butt instead of overlap. This prevents the batting from separating after use.

8. Turn one edge of backing under and hand-stitch in place.

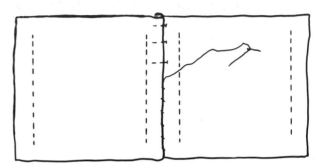

9. Sew blocks and lattice strips to fit across rows.

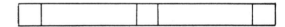

10. Place strip on first row of blocks, right sides together, matching small blocks to lattice strips. Stitch through all layers.

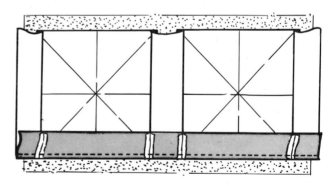

11. Continue to add lattice and quilted rows until block portion of quilt is complete.

12. Sew the border backing, right sides together, to the quilt backing. Sew sides first, then the ends. Do *not* stitch through the batting and top squares.

13. Attach the batting pieces to the batting in the quilted blocks using a loose overcast stitch.

14. Working on right side, pin and sew side pieces of first border. Stitch through *all* layers of the quilt. Turn side pieces right side up. Attach end pieces.

15. Continue adding borders in this manner.

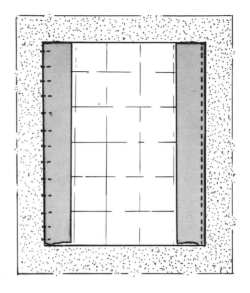

Hand Method

All of the various layouts may be used when hand-quilting.

1. Stop the quilting ½" from all edges. This provides the necessary room to machine stitch two top pieces together.

2. Construct finished blocks using the piecing diagrams for the unquilted top. Use the same construction as "Machine Method," except do *not* catch *any* backing or batting when joining blocks and lattice.

3. Quilt seams of block and lattice joinings.

4. A thimble is necessary. Try different kinds till you find one you can use comfortably.

5. The stitch itself requires practice: Start with a tiny knot. Enter the fabric about 1" from the first quilting stitch. Snap the thread just hard enough to pull the knot through the top layer, catching it in the batting.

With your free hand underneath the quilt, insert the needle straight down. As soon as your

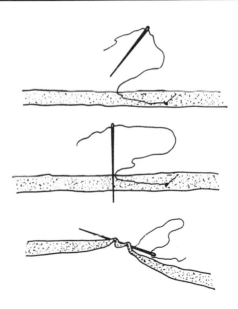

finger feels the point, "rock" the needle down, at the same time pushing the point up. Repeat these two motions, using your thumb (upper hand) to push the fabric over the point. To end a thread, take one or two tiny backstitches. Then come out about 1" away and cut thread short, leaving a 1" tail end anchored in the batting.

Any marking of quilting lines should be done just before the basting. Use a washable pen or fine chalk marker. (Pencil marks do *not* wash out).

In general, the less quilting done, the puffier your quilt will look. Extensive quilting will flatten an area.

10

COMPLETING THE QUILT

Binding the Edges

Binding the edges is the last step in creating a quilt. The quickest way is to turn the raw edge of the outer border to the back and stitch it in place. To do this the outer border must be cut 1³/₄″ wider than the finished width, allowing 1¹/₂″ for turnback. (All outer borders in this book include that extra width).

1. With right side up, trim off excess batting and backing so all edges are even with outer border edge.

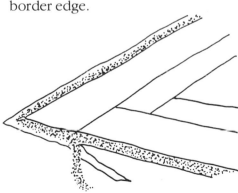

2. With back sides of quilt up, trim 1″ off backing and batting (do not cut off any border fabric).

Enjoying the fruits of labor.

49

3. Turn 1½" of border to the back of the quilt. You will be turning back ½" of the batting/backing also. This is necessary to retain a plump binding when quilt is used. Turn under ¾" of raw edge. Pin. Machine-stitch.

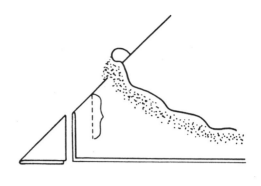

4. For easy mitered corners, on wrong side of border fabric only and using a Speedy, mark a 1½" square.

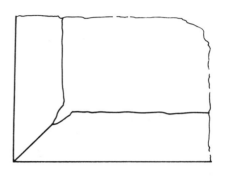

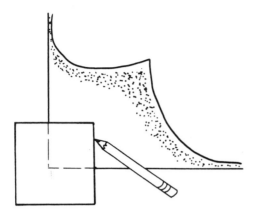

6. Turn ¾" under. Pin in place. Topstitch.

5. Right sides together, match the two lines. Stitch from fold line for ¾", backstitching both ends. Trim corner to a ½" seam. Turn to right side. Mitered corner will fall neatly in place, leaving ¾" free to turn under.

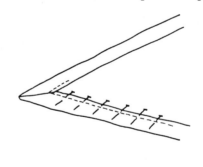

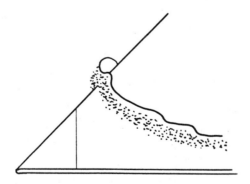

Carol Shafer, sampler in salmons and greens; 89 × 111,
View E, 14″ blocks on point, with 3″ lattice. Row 1: #51 —
Hour Glass; #66 — *Miller's Daughter;* #6 — *Paddle Wheel.*
Row 2: #32 — *Prairie Queen;* #93 — *Waving Palm.* Row 3:
#19 — *Party Hats;* #10 — *Card Trick;* #41 — *Graphically
Speaking.* Row 4: #63 — *Swing in the Center;* #85 — *Car-
ol's Cross.* Row 5: #17 — *Ribbons & Bows;* #46 — *May
Basket;* #3 — *Jack-in-the-Box.* Row 6: #53 — *Dutchman's
Puzzle;* #75 — *Peace.* Row 7: #4 — *Puerto Vallarta;* #76 —
Starry Paths; #65 — *Road to Oklahoma.*

Teresa Kline, blues on floral print; 59 × 76, View D, 12″ alternating blocks on point. #7—*Flight Pattern.*

Jan Eufer, *Baskets*, soft coral and green on white; 67 × 67, View D, 12″ alternating blocks on point. #46—*May Baskets.*

Helen Oelkrug, gray/pink on yellow; 69 × 83, View C, 12″ blocks with lattice. #69—Helen's Folly.

Ellie Bird, blue/wine on white print; 64 × 64, View B, 12″ blocks on point. #24—Shoo-Fly.

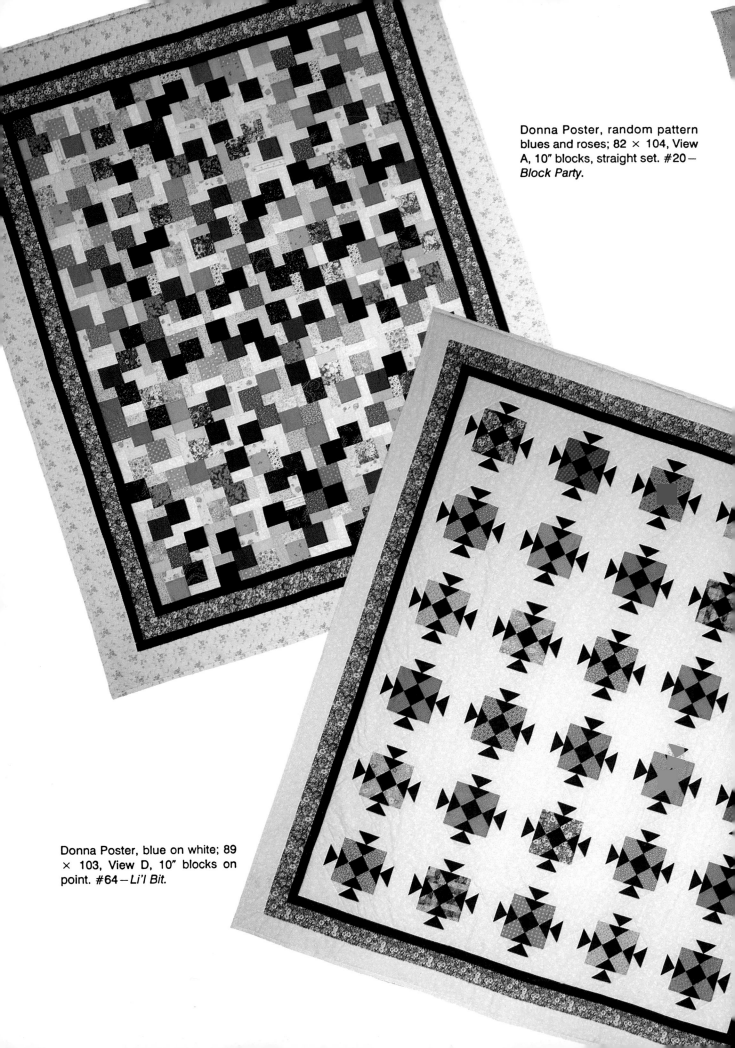

Donna Poster, random pattern
blues and roses; 82 × 104, View
A, 10″ blocks, straight set. #20—
Block Party.

Donna Poster, blue on white; 89
× 103, View D, 10″ blocks on
point. #64—*Li'l Bit.*

Ellie Bird, brown/black on white; 82 × 106, View A, 12″ blocks, straight set. #36—*Pathways*.

Tammy Peper, sampler in salmon and green, 48 × 48, View C, 12″ blocks with 3″ lattice. Row 1: #47—*Big Foot*; #81—*Off Beat*; #62—*Susannah Patch*. Row 2: #37—*Benedetto's First*; #42—*Introductions*; #73—*Clay's Choice*. Row 3: #77—*Windblown Star*; #56—*This 'n That*; #61—*Country Homes*.

Teresa Kline, aqua tones; 86 × 103, View D, 12″ alternating blocks on point. #22—*Square Deal*.

Shirley Campbell, gold, red and teal; 86 × 100, View A, 14″ blocks, straight set. #53—*Dutchman's Puzzle*.

Tammy Peper, reversed blocks in soft salmon and green; 45 × 45, View A, 12″ blocks, straight set. #12 — *Grandmother's Pride.*

Janet Jelen, pink and blue mosaic; 45 × 45, View A, 12″ blocks, straight set. #15 — *Jig-saw.*

Donna Poster, *Jewel Tones*; 61 × 81, View A, 10″ blocks, straight set. #34 — *Informal Diamonds.*

Caring for Your Quilt

Machine washing/drying: This works fine, provided you have used a bonded batting and have a washer and dryer large enough to accommodate your quilt. Use the gentlest cycle and a mild detergent. Use your dryer on delicate cycle *only. Never* use a dryer that is hot! Dry only to a slightly damp stage. Remove quilt and finish the drying process flat on a blanket or bed.

Hand washing/drying: Fill the bathtub half full of lukewarm water. Use a mild detergent. Squeeze gently and swish the quilt around in the water but never lift it while it is wet. The weight of the wet quilt at the bottom will snap the quilting threads. Rinse several times. Squeeze as much moisture from the quilt as possible. *Do not lift or wring.* When transporting a wet quilt, fold it into a bundle and carry it in your arms. Dry your quilt on a blanket spread out on a large flat surface, such as the floor in a spare bedroom. Outside on a sunny day works well, but be sure to put the top side of your quilt down to prevent fading.

Storage: Fold your quilt loosely and wrap it in a sheet or pillowcase. Never store it in plastic. Air must circulate around the quilt to preserve it.

APPENDICES

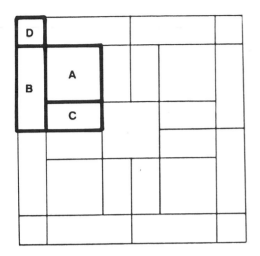

■		5/A + 4/D
▦		4/B + 4/C
▩		4/B + 4/C

1
"Santa Rosa"

BEGINNER

TEMPLATE NUMBERS

	10" block	12" block	14" block
A	41	43	12
B	108	104	109
C	87	88	89
D	36	37	32

BUILDING THE BLOCK

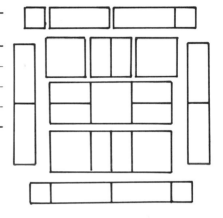

VARIATIONS

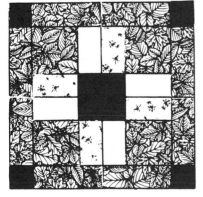

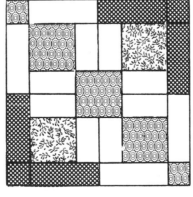

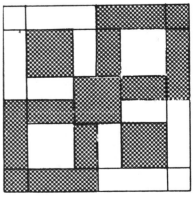

■	1/A + 4/D
▨	4/A + 8/B
▢	4/C
□	4/C

▦	4/B + 2/D
▨	3/A + 2/D
▧	2/A
□	4/B + 8/C

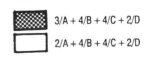

▦	3/A + 4/B + 4/C + 2/D
□	2/A + 4/B + 4/C + 2/D

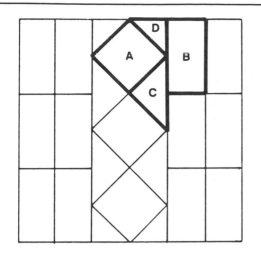
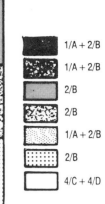
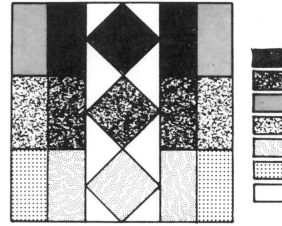

	1/A + 2/B
	1/A + 2/B
	2/B
	2/B
	1/A + 2/B
	2/B
	4/C + 4/D

2
"Formal Diamonds"

BEGINNER

TEMPLATE NUMBERS

	10" block	12" block	14" block
A	33	42	11
B	23	24	25
C	65	76	68
D	63	154	155

BUILDING THE BLOCK

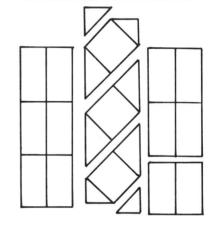

VARIATIONS

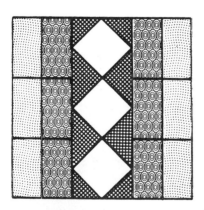

	4/C + 4/D
	6/B
	6/B
	3/A

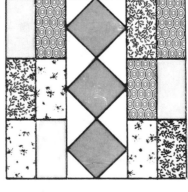

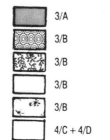

	3/A
	3/B
	3/B
	3/B
	3/B
	4/C + 4/D

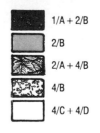

	1/A + 2/B
	2/B
	2/A + 4/B
	4/B
	4/C + 4/D

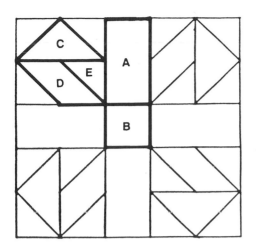

3
"Jack in the Box"

BEGINNER

TEMPLATE NUMBERS

	10" block	12" block	14" block
A	90	91	56
B	7	131	10
C	66	77	158
D	101	102	103
E	64	75	66

1/B + 4/D
16/E
4/A + 4/C

BUILDING THE BLOCK

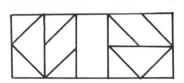

VARIATIONS

8/E
4/A + 8/E
1/B + 4/D
4/C

1/B + 16/E
4/A + 4/C + 4/D

1/B
4/A
4/C + 4/D
16/E

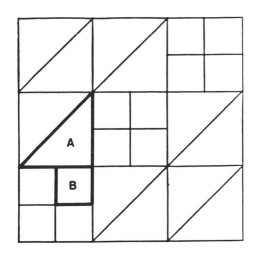

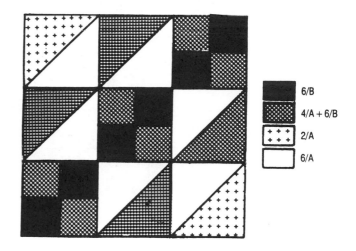

6/B
4/A + 6/B
2/A
6/A

4 "Puerto Vallarta"

BEGINNER

TEMPLATE NUMBERS

	10" block	12" block	14" block
A	68	70	83
B	6	39	40

BUILDING THE BLOCK

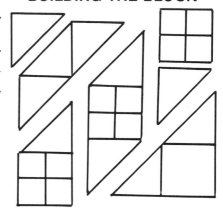

VARIATIONS

6/B
6/A
6/A + 6/B

2/A + 6/B
10/A
6/B

6/A + 6/B
6/A + 6/B

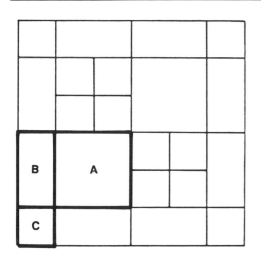

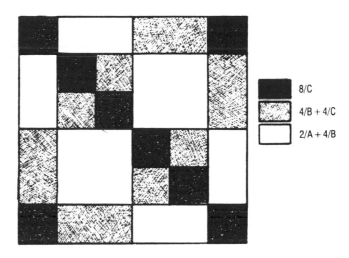

8/C

4/B + 4/C

2/A + 4/B

5
"French Cafe"

BEGINNER

TEMPLATE NUMBERS

	10" block	12" block	14" block
A	44	13	47
B	23	24	25
C	6	39	40

BUILDING THE BLOCK

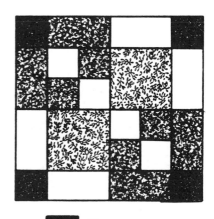

VARIATIONS

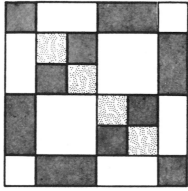

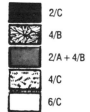

2/C

4/B

2/A + 4/B

4/C

6/C

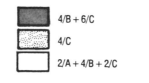

4/B + 6/C

4/C

2/A + 4/B + 2/C

4/C

4/B + 4/C

2/A

4/B + 4/C

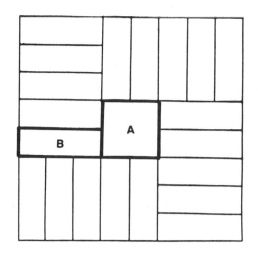

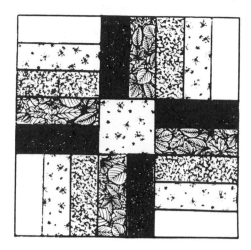

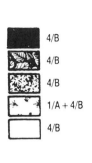

	4/B
	4/B
	4/B
	1/A + 4/B
	4/B

6
"Paddle Wheel"

BEGINNER

TEMPLATE NUMBERS

	10" block	12" block	14" block
A	41	43	12
B	108	104	109

BUILDING THE BLOCK

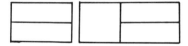

VARIATIONS

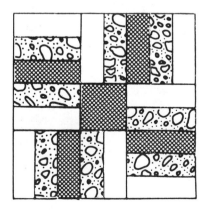

	1/A + 4/B
	8/B
	8/B

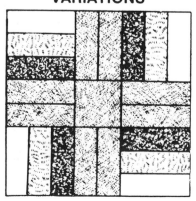

	4/B
	1/A + 8/B
	4/B
	4/B

	10/B
	6/B
	1/A + 4/B

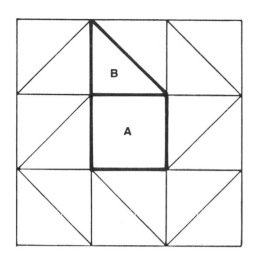

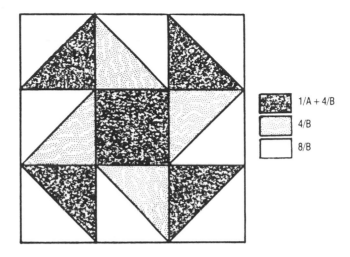

	1/A + 4/B
	4/B
	8/B

7
"Flight Pattern"

BEGINNER

TEMPLATE NUMBERS

	10" block	12" block	14" block
A	44	13	47
B	68	70	83

BUILDING THE BLOCK

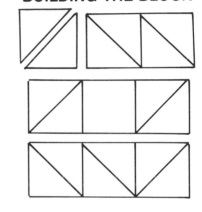

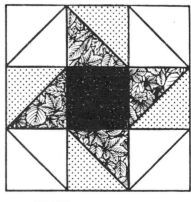

VARIATIONS

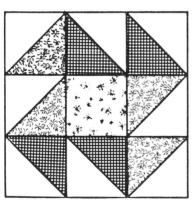

	4/B
	4/B
	1/A
	8/B

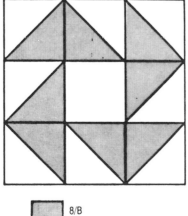

	8/B
	1/A + 8/B

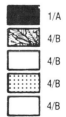

	1/A
	4/B
	4/B
	4/B
	4/B

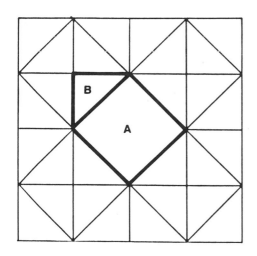

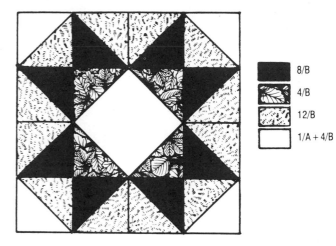

	8/B
	4/B
	12/B
	1/A + 4/B

8
"Tip Toes"

BEGINNER

TEMPLATE NUMBERS

	10" block	12" block	14" block
A	34	14	16
B	156	67	157

BUILDING THE BLOCK

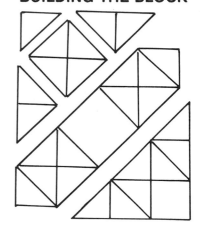

VARIATIONS

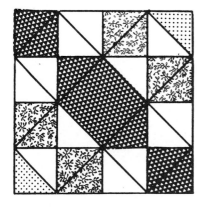

	1/A + 6/B
	8/B
	2/B
	12/B

	14/B
	1/A + 14/B

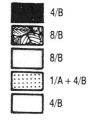

	4/B
	8/B
	8/B
	1/A + 4/B
	4/B

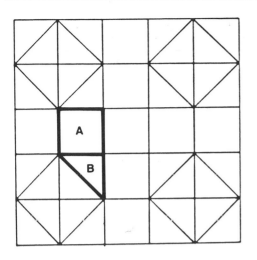

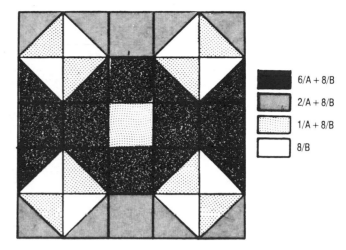

	6/A + 8/B
	2/A + 8/B
	1/A + 8/B
	8/B

TEMPLATE NUMBERS

	10″ block	12″ block	14″ block
A	7	131	10
B	64	75	66

9
"Box Seats"

BEGINNER

BUILDING THE BLOCK

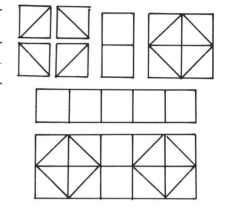

VARIATIONS

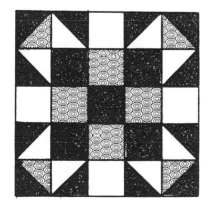

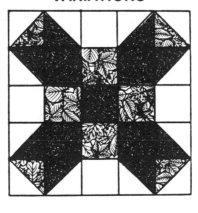

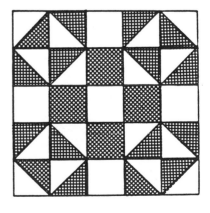

	1/A + 20/B
	4/A + 4/B
	4/A + 8/B

	1/A + 16/B
	4/A + 4/B
	4/A + 12/B

| | 4/A + 16/B |
| | 5/A + 16/B |

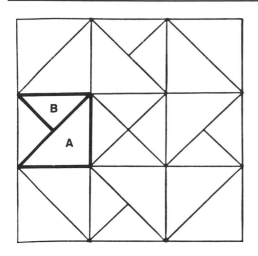

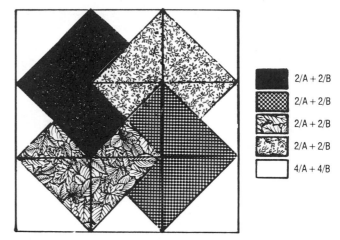

	2/A + 2/B
	2/A + 2/B
	2/A + 2/B
	2/A + 2/B
	4/A + 4/B

10
"Card Trick"

BEGINNER

TEMPLATE NUMBERS

	10" block	12" block	14" block
A	68	70	83
B	65	76	68

BUILDING THE BLOCK

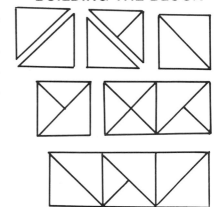

VARIATIONS

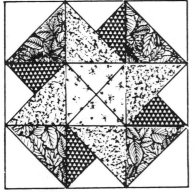

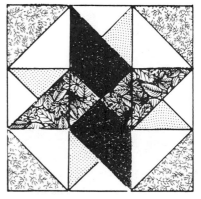

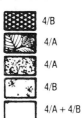

	4/B
	4/A
	4/A
	4/B
	4/A + 4/B

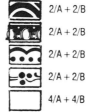

	2/A + 2/B
	2/A + 2/B
	2/A + 2/B
	2/A + 2/B
	4/A + 4/B

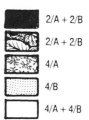

	2/A + 2/B
	2/A + 2/B
	4/A
	4/B
	4/A + 4/B

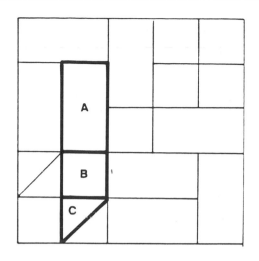

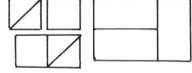

		2/C	
		5/B	
		2/C	
		2/A	
		2/A	
		2/B	
		4/A	

11
"Braid 'n' Bow"

BEGINNER

TEMPLATE NUMBERS

	10" block	12" block	14" block
A	90	91	56
B	7	131	10
C	64	75	66

BUILDING THE BLOCK

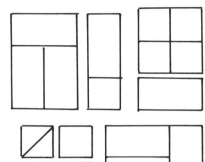

VARIATIONS

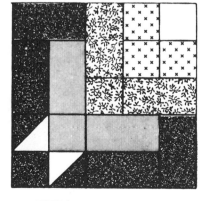

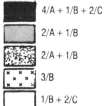

	4/A + 1/B + 2/C
	2/A + 1/B
	2/A + 1/B
	3/B
	1/B + 2/C

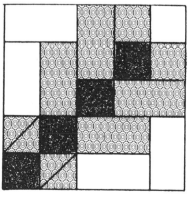

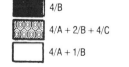

	4/B
	4/A + 2/B + 4/C
	4/A + 1/B

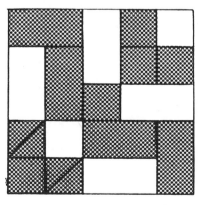

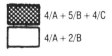

	4/A + 5/B + 4/C
	4/A + 2/B

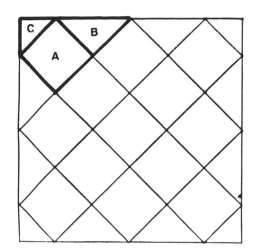

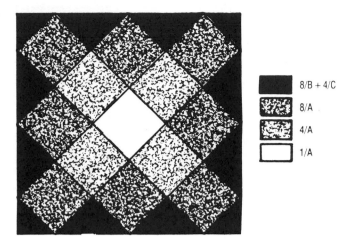

	8/B + 4/C
	8/A
	4/A
	1/A

TEMPLATE NUMBERS

	10" block	12" block	14" block
A	33	42	11
B	65	76	68
C	63	154	155

12 "Grandmother's Pride"

BEGINNER

BUILDING THE BLOCK

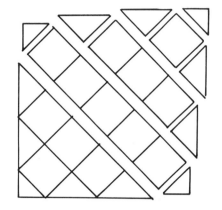

VARIATIONS

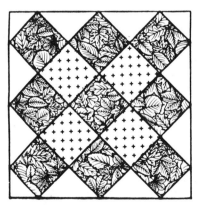

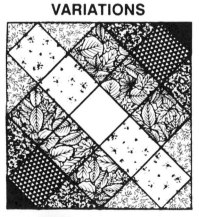

	9/A
	4/A
	8/B + 4/C

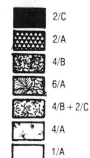

	2/C
	2/A
	4/B
	6/A
	4/B + 2/C
	4/A
	1/A

| | 9/A |
| | 4/A + 8/B + 4/C |

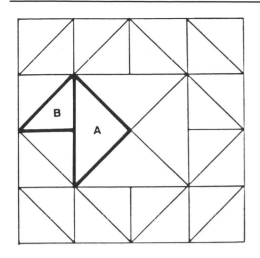

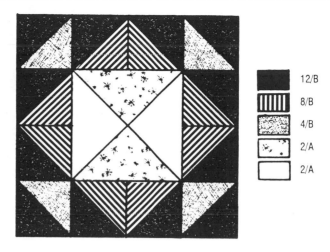

	12/B
	8/B
	4/B
	2/A
	2/A

13
"3:00 A.M."

BEGINNER

TEMPLATE NUMBERS

	10" block	12" block	14" block
A	69	71	84
B	156	67	157

BUILDING THE BLOCK

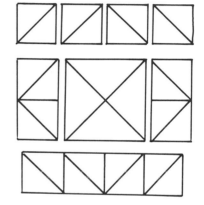

VARIATIONS

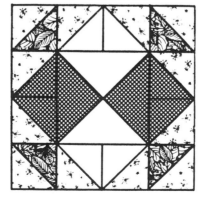

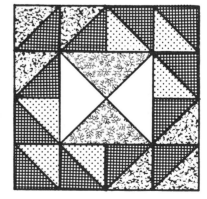

	8/B
	4/B
	8/B
	4/A
	4/B

	2/A + 4/B
	4/B
	12/B
	2/A + 4/B

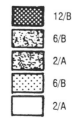

	12/B
	6/B
	2/A
	6/B
	2/A

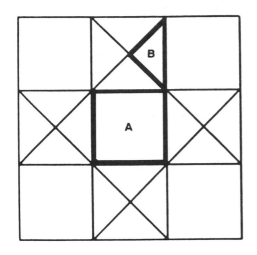

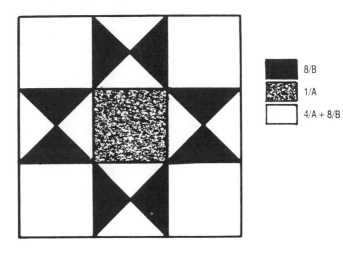

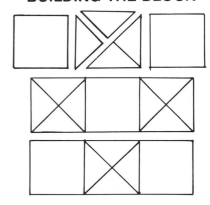

| 8/B |
| 1/A |
| 4/A + 8/B |

14
"Ohio Star"

BEGINNER

TEMPLATE NUMBERS

	10" block	12" block	14" block
A	44	13	47
B	65	76	68

BUILDING THE BLOCK

VARIATIONS

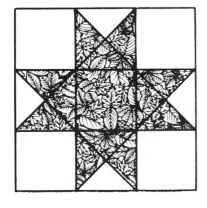

| 1/A + 12/B |
| 4/A + 4/B |

| 8/B |
| 5/A |
| 8/B |

| 1/A + 8/B |
| 4/A + 8/B |

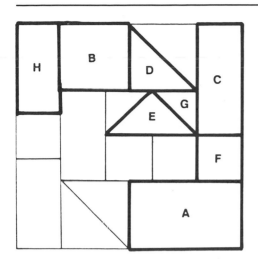

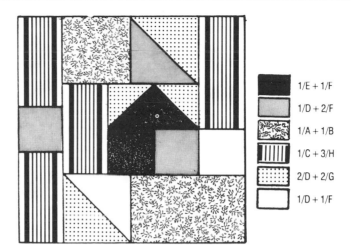

■	1/E + 1/F	
	1/D + 2/F	
	1/A + 1/B	
‖‖	1/C + 3/H	
	2/D + 2/G	
	1/D + 1/F	

15 "Jigsaw"

BEGINNER

TEMPLATE NUMBERS

	10" block	12" block	14" block
A	92	93	94
B	43	45	46
C	105	106	107
D	67	78	81
E	66	77	158
F	7	131	10
G	64	75	66
H	90	91	56

BUILDING THE BLOCK

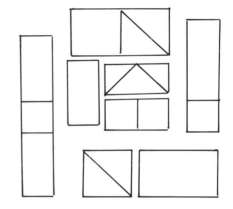

VARIATIONS

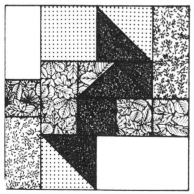

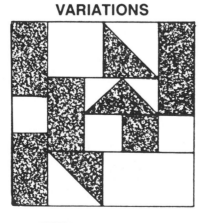

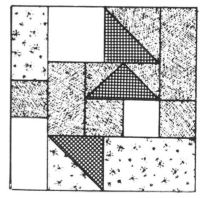

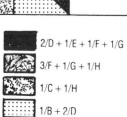

■	2/D + 1/E + 1/F + 1/G
	3/F + 1/G + 1/H
	1/C + 1/H
	1/B + 2/D
	1/A + 1/H

	1/C + 2/D + 1/E + 1/F + 3/H
	1/A + 1/B + 2/D + 3/F + 2/G

	2/D + 1/E
	1/C + 1/D + 3/F + 2/G + 1/H
	1/A + 1/D + 1/H
	1/B + 1/F + 1/H

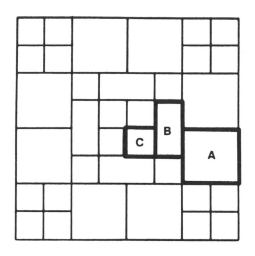

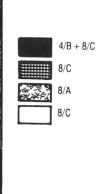

	4/B + 8/C
	8/C
	8/A
	8/C

16
"Criss-Cross"

BEGINNER

TEMPLATE NUMBERS

	10" block	12" block	14" block
A	41	43	12
B	87	88	89
C	36	37	32

BUILDING THE BLOCK

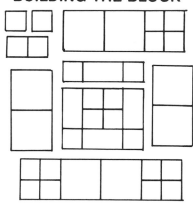

VARIATIONS

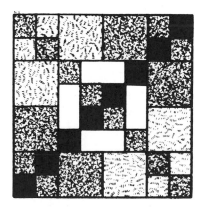

	8/C
	4/A + 12/C
	4/A + 4/C
	4/B

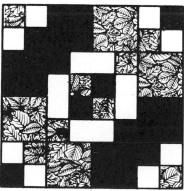

	4/A + 8/C
	4/A + 8/C
	4/B + 8/C

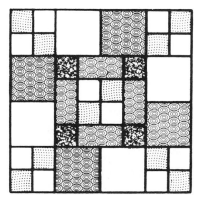

	4/C
	4/A + 4/B
	10/C
	4/A + 10/C

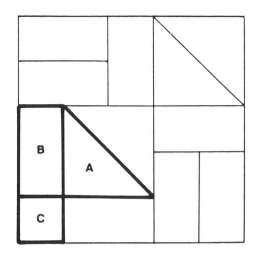

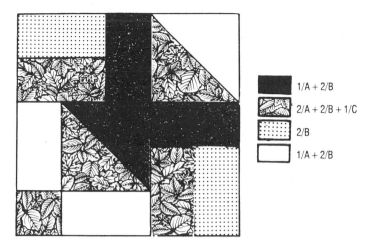

- ■ 1/A + 2/B
- 2/A + 2/B + 1/C
- 2/B
- 1/A + 2/B

TEMPLATE NUMBERS

	10" block	12" block	14" block
A	80	72	86
B	90	91	56
C	7	131	10

17
"Ribbons & Bows"

BEGINNER

BUILDING THE BLOCK

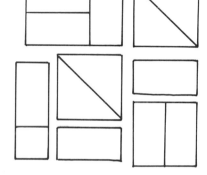

VARIATIONS

- 6/B
- 2/A + 1/C
- 2/A + 2/B

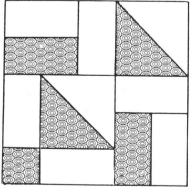

- 2/A + 2/B + 1/C
- 2/A + 6/B

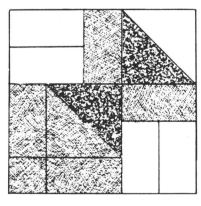

- 2/A
- 1/A + 4/B + 1/C
- 1/A + 4/B

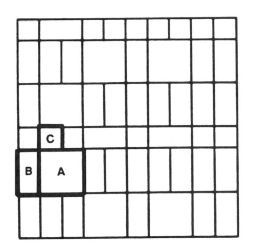

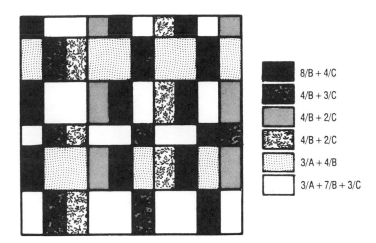

	8/B + 4/C
	4/B + 3/C
	4/B + 2/C
	4/B + 2/C
	3/A + 4/B
	3/A + 7/B + 3/C

18 "Plaid"

BEGINNER

TEMPLATE NUMBERS

	10" block	12" block	14" block
A	7	131	10
B	51	52	53
C	35	4	31

BUILDING THE BLOCK

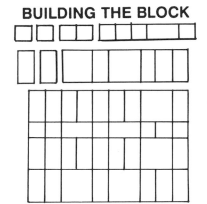

VARIATIONS

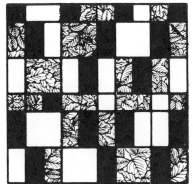

	15/B + 4/C
	5/A + 6/B + 5/C
	1/A + 10/B + 5/C

	12/B + 5/C
	3/A + 10/B + 6/C
	3/A + 9/B + 3/C

	6/A + 10/B + 4/C
	6B + 4/C
	15B + 6/C

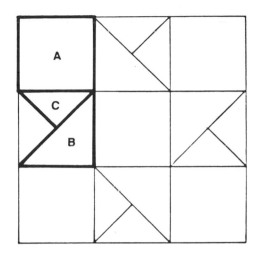

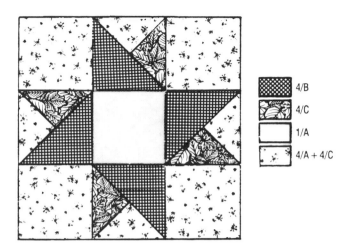

			4/B
			4/C
			1/A
			4/A + 4/C

19
"Party Hats"

BEGINNER

TEMPLATE NUMBERS

	10" block	12" block	14" block
A	44	13	47
B	68	70	83
C	65	76	68

BUILDING THE BLOCK

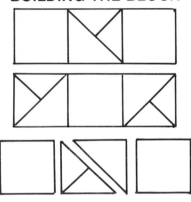

VARIATIONS

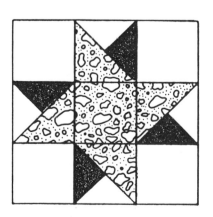

	4/C
	1/A + 4/B
	4/A + 4/C

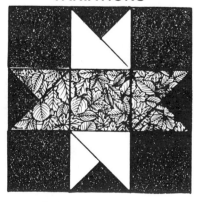

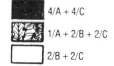

	4/A + 4/C
	1/A + 2/B + 2/C
	2/B + 2/C

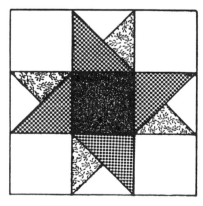

	1/A
	4/B
	4/C
	4/A + 4/C

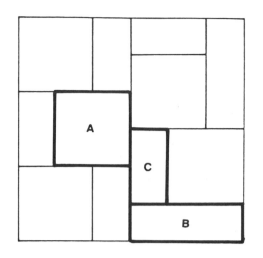

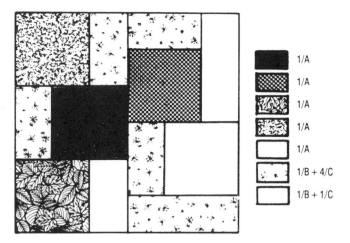

	1/A
	1/A
	1/A
	1/A
	1/A
	1/B + 4/C
	1/B + 1/C

20
"Block Party"

___

BEGINNER

TEMPLATE NUMBERS

	10" block	12" block	14" block
A	44	13	47
B	19	110	111
C	23	24	25

BUILDING THE BLOCK

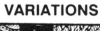

VARIATIONS

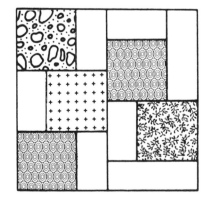

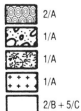

	2/A
	1/A
	1/A
	1/A
	2/B + 5/C

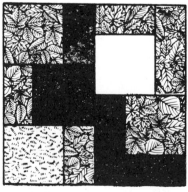

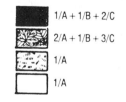

	1/A + 1/B + 2/C
	2/A + 1/B + 3/C
	1/A
	1/A

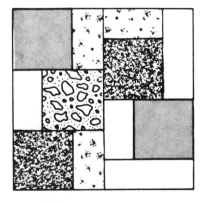

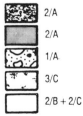

	2/A
	2/A
	1/A
	3/C
	2/B + 2/C

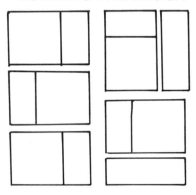

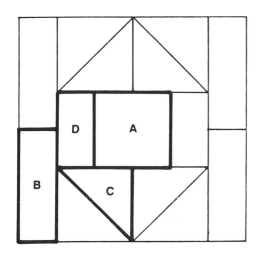

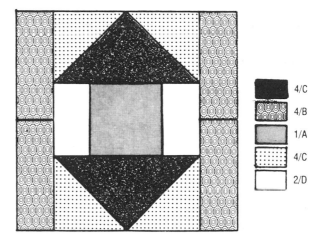

	4/C
	4/B
	1/A
	4/C
	2/D

21 "Rockets"

BEGINNER

TEMPLATE NUMBERS

	10" block	12" block	14" block
A	44	13	47
B	19	110	111
C	68	70	83
D	23	24	25

BUILDING THE BLOCK

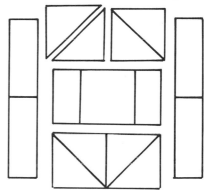

VARIATIONS

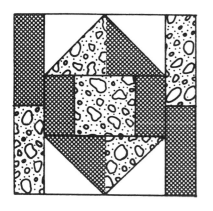

	2/B + 2/C + 2/D
	1/A + 2/B + 2/C
	4/C

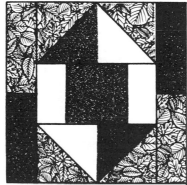

	1/A + 2/B + 2/C
	2/B + 4/C
	2/C + 2/D

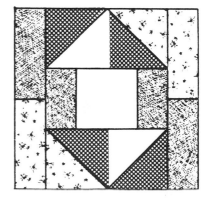

	4/C
	2/B + 2/D
	2/B + 2/C
	1/A + 2/C

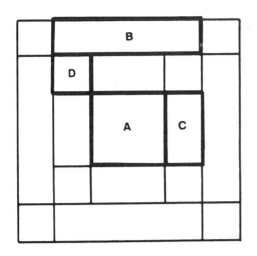

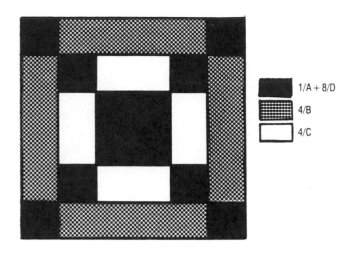

			1/A + 8/D
			4/B
			4/C

22
"Square Deal"

BEGINNER

TEMPLATE NUMBERS

	10" block	12" block	14" block
A	44	13	47
B	118	120	121
C	23	24	25
D	6	39	40

BUILDING THE BLOCK

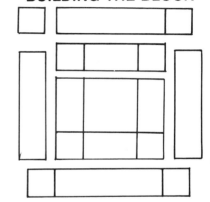

VARIATIONS

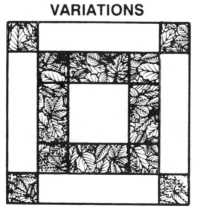

	1/A + 4/B
	4/C + 8/D

	4/C + 8/D
	1/A + 4/B

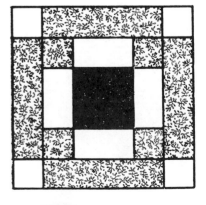

	1/A
	4/B + 4/D
	4/C + 4/D

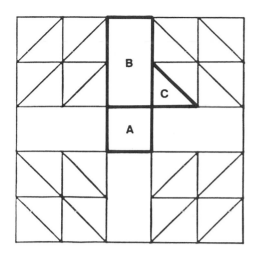

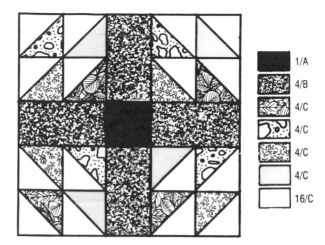

	1/A
	4/B
	4/C
	4/C
	4/C
	4/C
	16/C

23
"Handy Andy"

BEGINNER

TEMPLATE NUMBERS

	10" block	12" block	14" block
A	7	131	10
B	90	91	56
C	64	75	66

BUILDING THE BLOCK

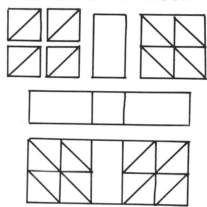

VARIATIONS

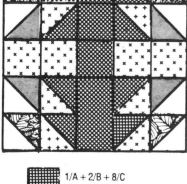

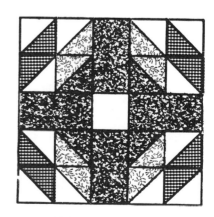

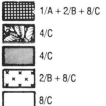

	1/A + 2/B + 8/C
	4/C
	4/C
	2/B + 8/C
	8/C

| | 1/A + 16/C |
| | 4/B + 16C |

	4/B + 4/C
	8/C
	8/C
	1/A + 12/C

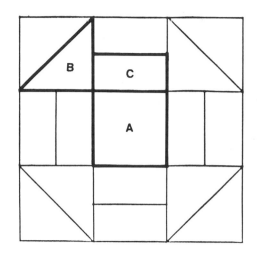

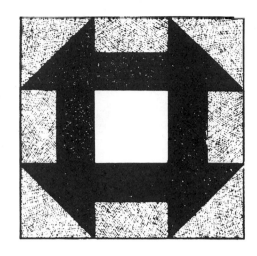

4/B + 4/C
4/B + 4/C
1/A

24 "Shoo-Fly"

BEGINNER

TEMPLATE NUMBERS

	10" block	12" block	14" block
A	44	13	47
B	68	70	83
C	23	24	25

BUILDING THE BLOCK

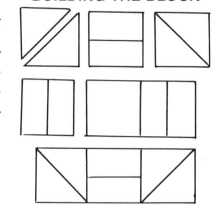

VARIATIONS

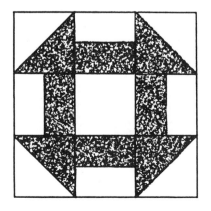

4/B + 4/C
1/A + 4/B + 4/C

4/B + 4/C
4/B + 4C
1/A

1/A + 4/C
4/B
4/B + 4/C

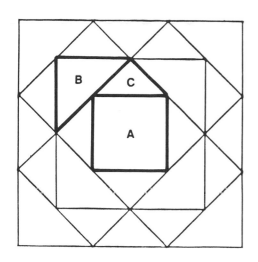

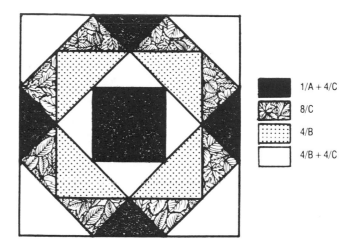

■		1/A + 4/C
▨		8/C
▦		4/B
□		4/B + 4/C

25 "Gentleman's Fancy"

BEGINNER

TEMPLATE NUMBERS

	10" block	12" block	14" block
A	44	13	47
B	68	70	83
C	65	76	68

BUILDING THE BLOCK

VARIATIONS

▨	4/B + 8/C
▦	8/C
□	1/A + 4/B

▨	16/C
□	1/A + 8/B

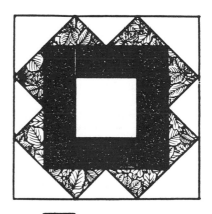

■	4/B + 4/C
▨	8/C
□	1/A + 4/B + 4/C

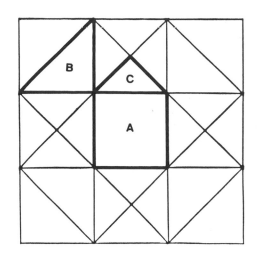

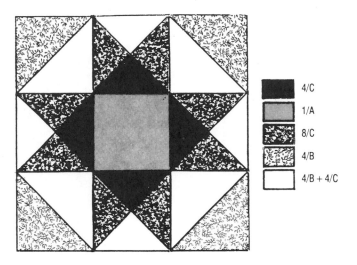

	4/C
	1/A
	8/C
	4/B
	4/B + 4/C

26
"Four-X"

BEGINNER

TEMPLATE NUMBERS

	10" block	12" block	14" block
A	44	13	47
B	68	70	83
C	65	76	68

BUILDING THE BLOCK

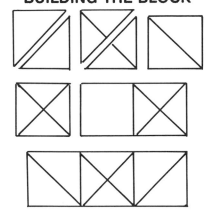

VARIATIONS

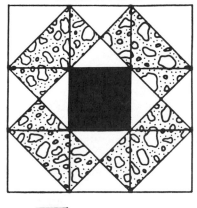

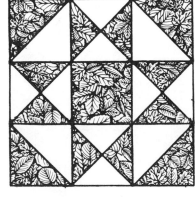

	8/C
	1/A
	8/B + 8/C

	1/A
	4/B + 8/C
	4/B + 8/C

	1/A + 4/B + 8/C
	4/B + 8/C

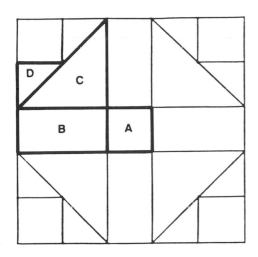

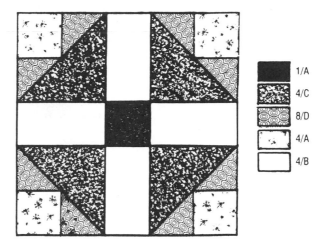

	1/A
	4/C
	8/D
	4/A
	4/B

27
"Cross & Crown"

BEGINNER

TEMPLATE NUMBERS

	10" block	12" block	14" block
A	7	131	10
B	90	91	56
C	80	72	86
D	64	75	66

BUILDING THE BLOCK

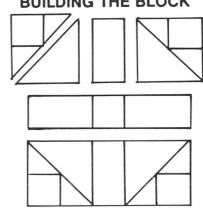

VARIATIONS

	1/A + 4/B
	4/A
	4/C + 8/D

	1/A + 8/D
	4/C
	4/A + 4/B

| | 5/A + 4/C |
| | 4/B + 8/D |

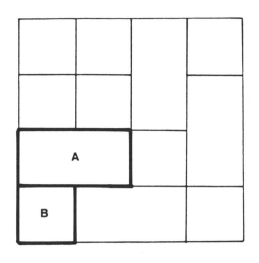

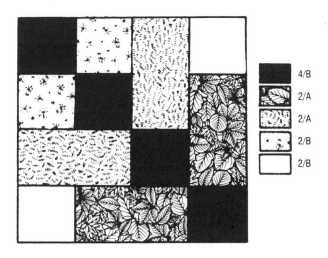

	4/B
	2/A
	2/A
	2/B
	2/B

28
"Broken Bricks"

BEGINNER

TEMPLATE NUMBERS

	10" block	12" block	14" block
A	55	57	58
B	41	43	12

BUILDING THE BLOCK

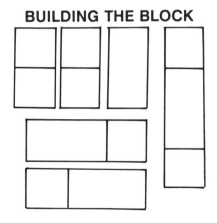

VARIATIONS

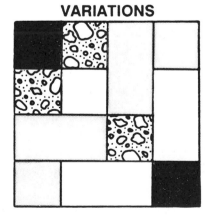

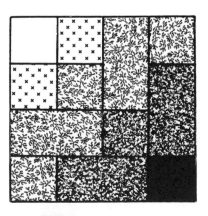

	2/A + 1/B
	2/A + 1/B
	6/B

	2/B
	3/B
	2/A + 2/B
	2/A + 1/B

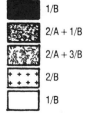

	1/B
	2/A + 1/B
	2/A + 3/B
	2/B
	1/B

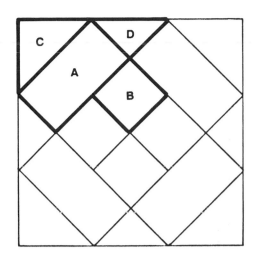

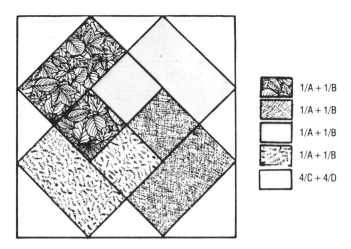

	1/A + 1/B
	1/A + 1/B
	1/A + 1/B
	1/A + 1/B
	4/C + 4/D

29 "Easy Card Trick"

BEGINNER

TEMPLATE NUMBERS

	10″ block	12″ block	14″ block
A	54	26	27
B	33	42	11
C	68	70	83
D	65	76	68

BUILDING THE BLOCK

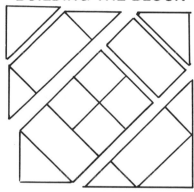

VARIATIONS

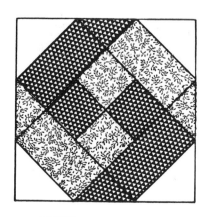

	2/A + 2/B + 2/D
	2/A + 2/B + 2/D
	4/C

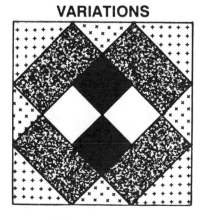

	2/B
	4/A
	4/C + 4/D
	2/B

	4/C + 4/D
	2/A + 2/B
	2/A + 2/B

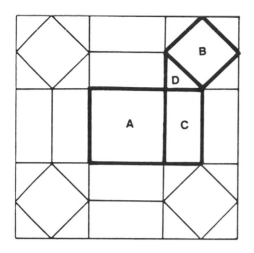

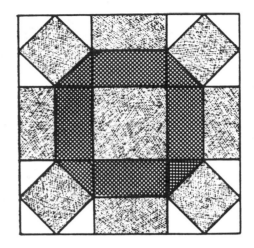

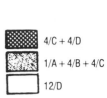

4/C + 4/D

1/A + 4/B + 4/C

12/D

30
"Stained Glass"

BEGINNER

TEMPLATE NUMBERS

	10" block	12" block	14" block
A	44	13	47
B	33	42	11
C	23	24	25
D	63	154	155

BUILDING THE BLOCK

VARIATIONS

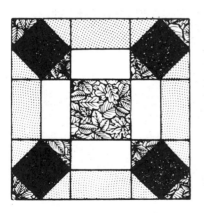

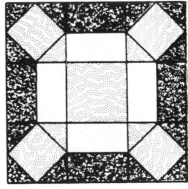

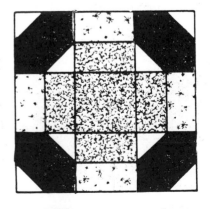

4/B

4/C + 8/D

1/A + 8/D

4/C

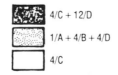

4/C + 12/D

1/A + 4/B + 4/D

4/C

4/B + 8/D

1/A + 4/C

4/C

8/D

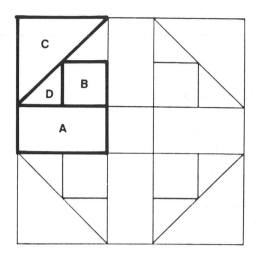

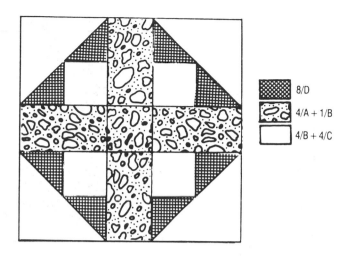

	8/D
	4/A + 1/B
	4/B + 4/C

31
"Switch"

BEGINNER

TEMPLATE NUMBERS

	10" block	12" block	14" block
A	90	91	56
B	7	131	10
C	80	72	86
D	64	75	66

BUILDING THE BLOCK

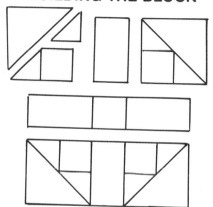

VARIATIONS

	4/A
	1/B + 4/C + 8/D
	4/B

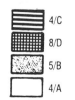

	4/C
	8/D
	5/B
	4/A

	5/B + 4/C
	4/A + 8/D

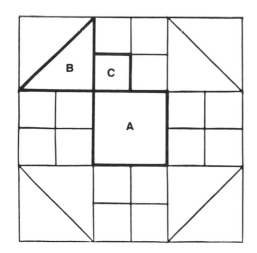

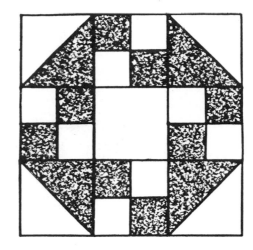

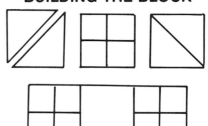

4/B + 8/C

1/A + 4/B + 8/C

32
"Prairie Queen"

BEGINNER

TEMPLATE NUMBERS

	10" block	12" block	14" block
A	44	13	47
B	68	70	83
C	6	39	40

BUILDING THE BLOCK

VARIATIONS

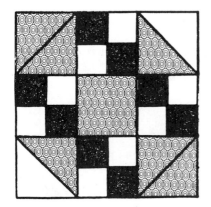

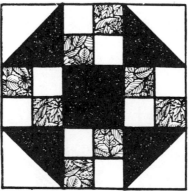

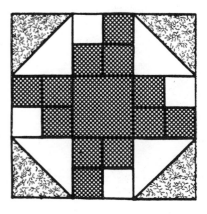

8/C
1/A + 6/B
2/B + 8/C

1/A + 4/B
8/C
4/B + 8/C

1/A + 12/C
4/B
4/B + 4/C

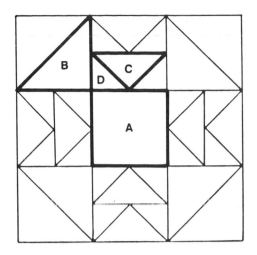

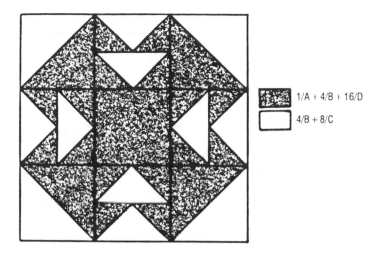

| 1/A + 4/B + 16/D |
| 4/B + 8/C |

33 "Four Ts"

BEGINNER

TEMPLATE NUMBERS

	10" block	12" block	14" block
A	44	13	47
B	68	70	83
C	65	76	68
D	63	154	155

BUILDING THE BLOCK

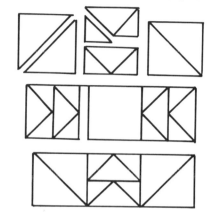

VARIATIONS

| 16/D |
| 4/B + 4/C |
| 1/A + 4/C |
| 4/B |

| 1/A + 8/C |
| 4/B |
| 4/B + 16/D |

| 4/B + 4/C |
| 4/C |
| 1/A + 8/D |
| 4/B + 8/D |

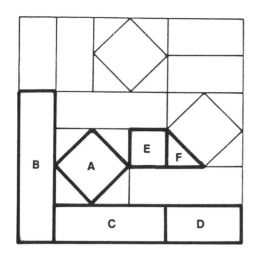

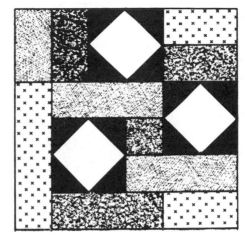

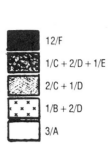

12/F

1/C + 2/D + 1/E

2/C + 1/D

1/B + 2/D

3/A

34 "Informal Diamonds"

INTERMEDIATE

TEMPLATE NUMBERS

	10" block	12" block	14" block
A	33	42	11
B	118	120	121
C	19	110	111
D	23	24	25
E	6	39	40
F	63	154	155

BUILDING THE BLOCK

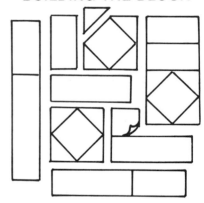

VARIATIONS

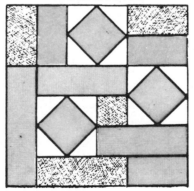

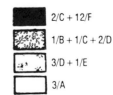

3/A + 2/D + 1/E + 6/F

1/B + 2/C + 1/D

1/C + 2/D

6/F

3/A + 1/B + 2/C + 3/D

1/C + 2/D + 1/E

12/F

2/C + 12/F

1/B + 1/C + 2/D

3/D + 1/E

3/A

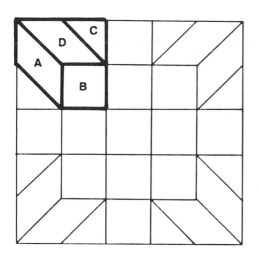

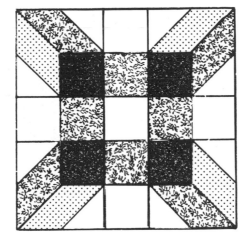

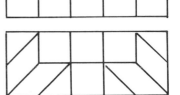

4/B

4/B + 4/D

4/A

5/B + 8/C

BUILDING THE BLOCK

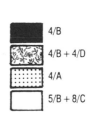

TEMPLATE NUMBERS

	10" block	12" block	14" block
A	101	102	103
B	7	131	10
C	64	75	66
D	177	178	179

35
"High Noon"

INTERMEDIATE

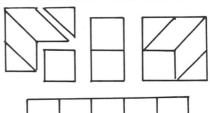

VARIATIONS

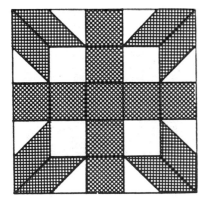

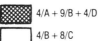 4/A + 9/B + 4/D

4/B + 8/C

 4/A + 4/D

8/B

4/B

1/B + 8/C

 5/B + 8/C

8/B

4/A + 4/D

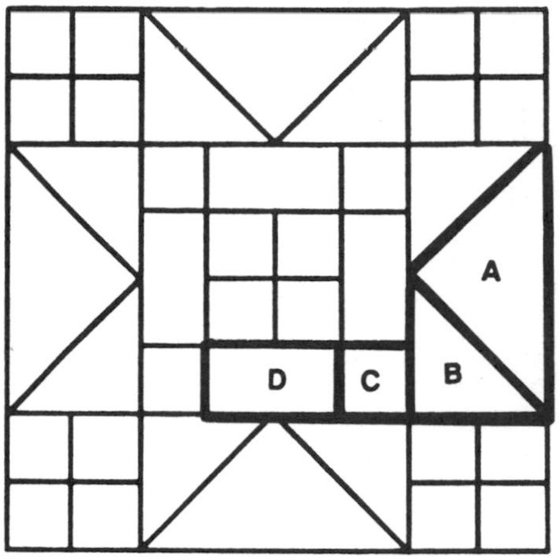
A
D
C
B

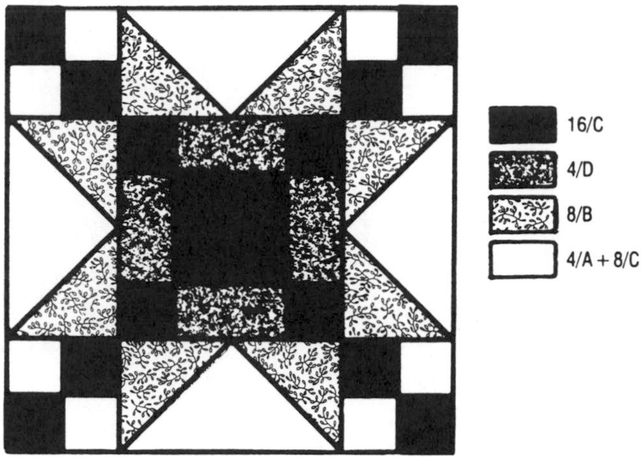
16/C
4/D
8/B
4/A + 8/C

36
"Pathways"

INTERMEDIATE

TEMPLATE NUMBERS

	10" block	12" block	14" block
A	69	71	84
B	156	67	157
C	36	37	32
D	87	88	89

BUILDING THE BLOCK

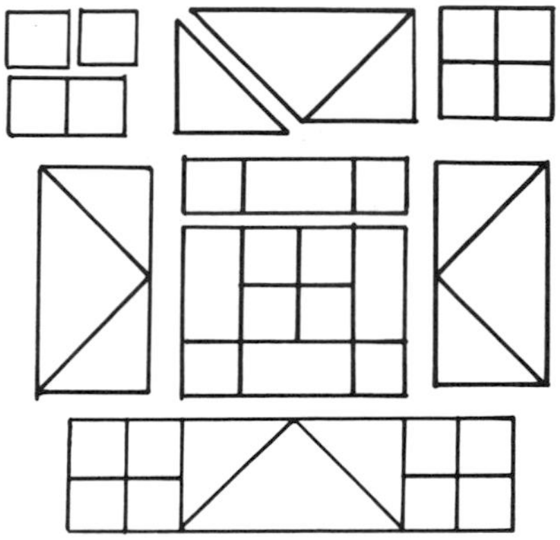

VARIATIONS

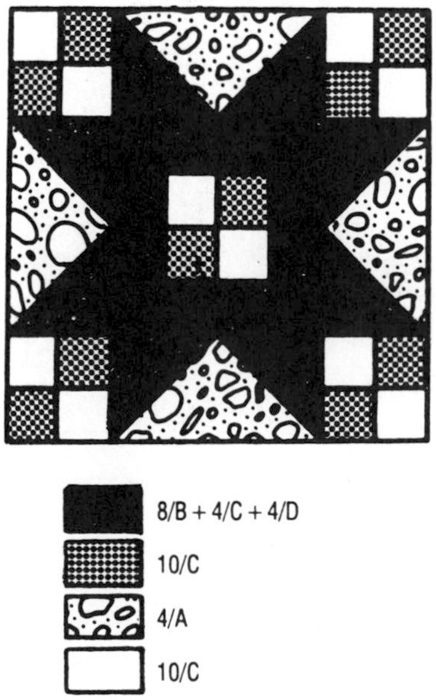
8/B + 4/C + 4/D
10/C
4/A
10/C

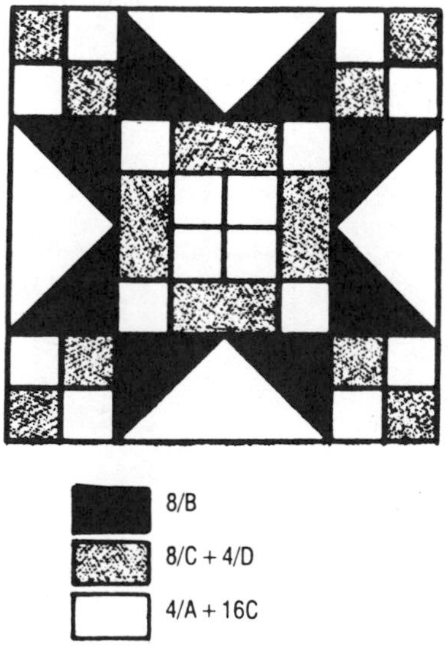
8/B
8/C + 4/D
4/A + 16C

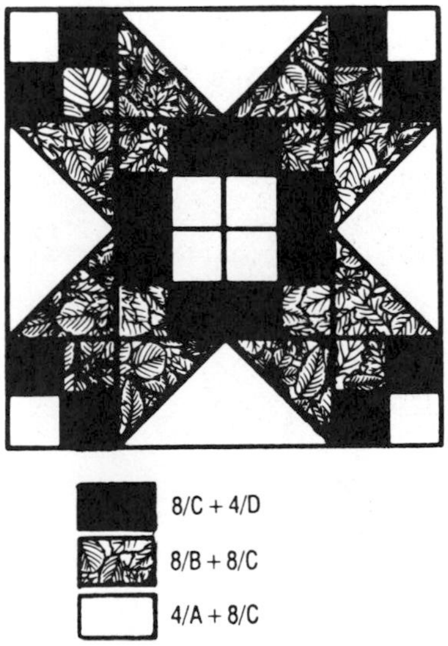
8/C + 4/D
8/B + 8/C
4/A + 8/C

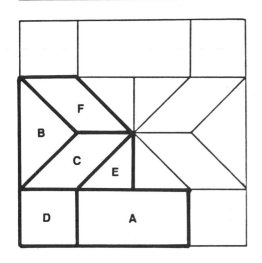

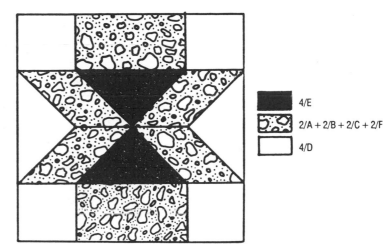

	4/E
	2/A + 2/B + 2/C + 2/F
	4/D

37 "Benedetto's First"

INTERMEDIATE

TEMPLATE NUMBERS

	10" block	12" block	14" block
A	55	57	58
B	69	71	84
C	201	202	203
D	41	43	12
E	156	67	157
F	162	163	164

BUILDING THE BLOCK

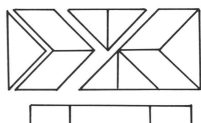

VARIATIONS

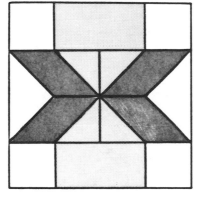

	2/E + 2/F
	2/B + 4/D
	2/A
	2/C + 2/E

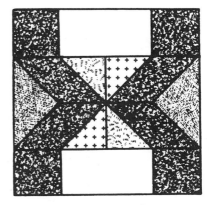

	2/C + 2/F
	2/A + 4/E
	2/B + 4/D

	2/C + 4/D + 2/F
	2/B
	2/E
	2/E
	2/A

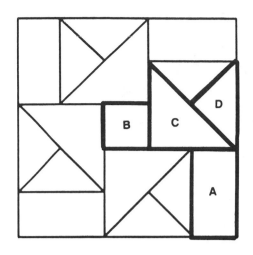

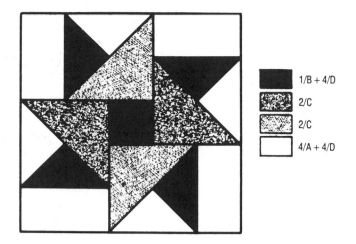

1/B + 4/D

2/C

2/C

4/A + 4/D

38
"Chasing Tails"

INTERMEDIATE

TEMPLATE NUMBERS

	10" block	12" block	14" block
A	90	91	56
B	7	131	10
C	80	72	86
D	66	77	158

BUILDING THE BLOCK

VARIATIONS

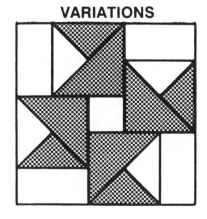

 2/C + 2/D

4/A + 1/B + 4/D

2/C + 2/D

4/C + 4/D

4/A + 1/B + 4/D

 1/B

4/A + 4/D

4/C

4/D

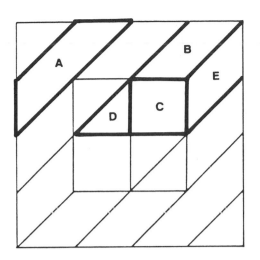

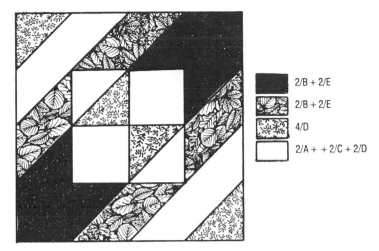

	2/B + 2/E
	2/B + 2/E
	4/D
	2/A + + 2/C + 2/D

39
"Hidden Star"

INTERMEDIATE

TEMPLATE NUMBERS

	10" block	12" block	14" block
A	187	189	191
B	201	202	203
C	41	43	12
D	156	67	157
E	162	163	164

BUILDING THE BLOCK

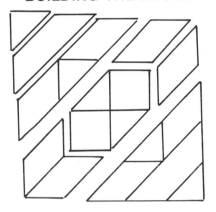

VARIATIONS

	2/B + 2/D + 2/E
	2/A + 2/E
	2/B + 2/D
	2/C + 2/D

	2/C + 2/D
	2/A + 2/B + 2/D + 2/E
	2/B + 2/E
	2/D

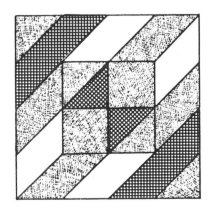

	2/A + 2/D
	2/B + 2/C + 4/D + 2/E
	2/B + 2/E

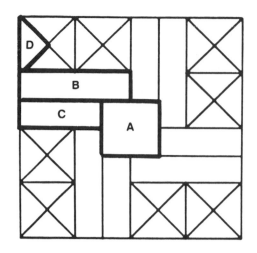

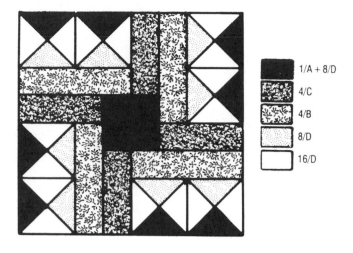

			1/A + 8/D
			4/C
			4/B
			8/D
			16/D

40 "Tumblers"

INTERMEDIATE

TEMPLATE NUMBERS

	10" block	12" block	14" block
A	41	43	12
B	115	117	119
C	108	104	109
D	153	74	75

BUILDING THE BLOCK

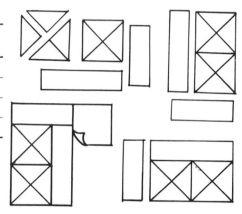

VARIATIONS

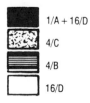

	1/A + 16/D
	4/C
	4/B
	16/D

	1/A + 4/B + 16/D
	4/C + 16/D

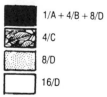

	1/A + 4/B + 8/D
	4/C
	8/D
	16/D

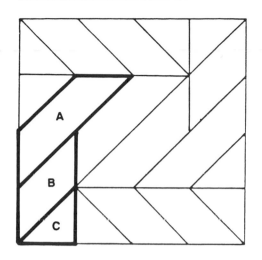

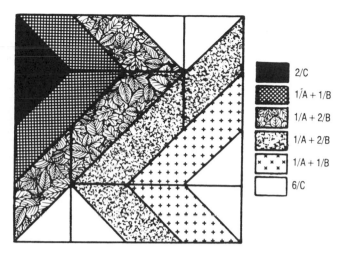

	2/C
	1/A + 1/B
	1/A + 2/B
	1/A + 2/B
	1/A + 1/B
	6/C

41 "Graphically Speaking"

INTERMEDIATE

TEMPLATE NUMBERS

	10" block	12" block	14" block
A	187	189	191
B	162	163	164
C	156	67	157

BUILDING THE BLOCK

VARIATIONS

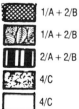

	1/A + 2/B
	1/A + 2/B
	2/A + 2/B
	4/C
	4/C

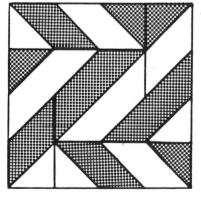

	2/A + 3/B + 4/C
	2/A + 3/B + 4/C

	2/B + 8/C
	2/A + 2/B
	2/A + 2/B

95

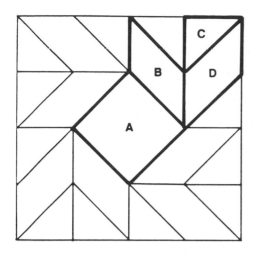

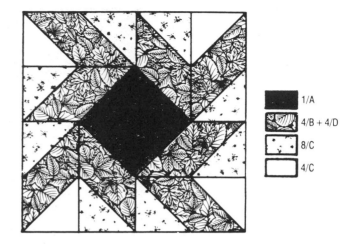

	1/A
	4/B + 4/D
	8/C
	4/C

42
"Introductions"

INTERMEDIATE

	10" block	12" block	14" block
A	34	14	16
B	201	202	203
C	156	67	157
D	162	163	164

BUILDING THE BLOCK

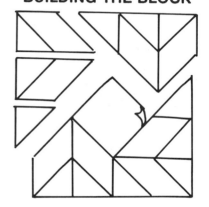

VARIATIONS

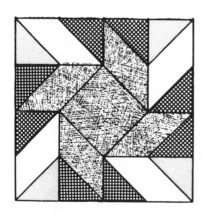

	8/C
	1/A + 4/B
	4/C
	4/D

	1/A + 12/C
	4/B + 4/D

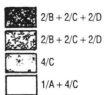

	2/B + 2/C + 2/D
	2/B + 2/C + 2/D
	4/C
	1/A + 4/C

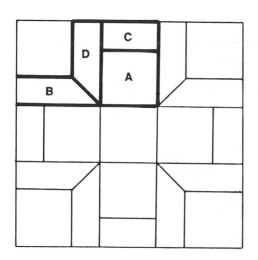

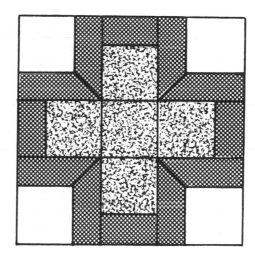

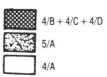

4/B + 4/C + 4/D

5/A

4/A

43 "Lunchtime"

INTERMEDIATE

TEMPLATE NUMBERS

	10" block	12" block	14" block
A	41	43	12
B	95	96	97
C	87	88	89
D	171	172	173

BUILDING THE BLOCK

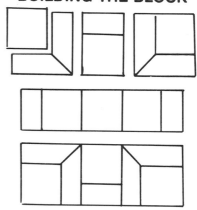

VARIATIONS

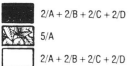

2/A + 2/B + 2/C + 2/D

5/A

2/A + 2/B + 2/C + 2/D

3/A

2/A + 2/C

4/A + 2/C

4/B + 4/D

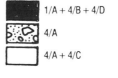

1/A + 4/B + 4/D

4/A

4/A + 4/C

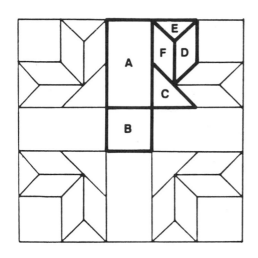

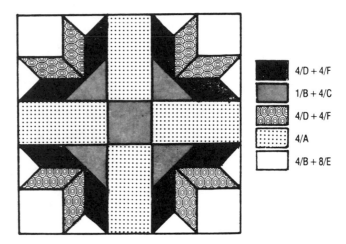

4/D + 4/F
1/B + 4/C
4/D + 4/F
4/A
4/B + 8/E

44
"Blossoms"

INTERMEDIATE

TEMPLATE NUMBERS

	10" block	12" block	14" block
A	90	91	56
B	7	131	10
C	64	75	66
D	216	217	218
E	62	73	64
F	159	160	161

BUILDING THE BLOCK

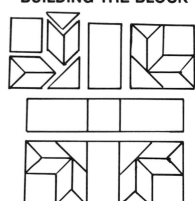

VARIATIONS

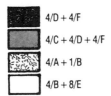
4/D + 4/F
4/C + 4/D + 4/F
4/A + 1/B
4/B + 8/E

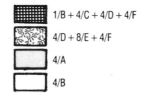
1/B + 4/C + 4/D + 4/F
4/D + 8/E + 4/F
4/A
4/B

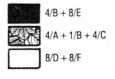
4/B + 8/E
4/A + 1/B + 4/C
8/D + 8/F

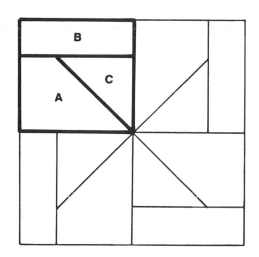

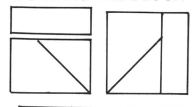

		4/C
		4/B
		4/A

45
"Water Wheel"

INTERMEDIATE

TEMPLATE NUMBERS

	10" block	12" block	14" block
A	138	139	140
B	19	110	111
C	68	70	83

BUILDING THE BLOCK

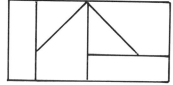

VARIATIONS

	4/B + 4/C
	4/A

	4/B
	2/A + 2/C
	2/A + 2/C

	4/A
	4/B
	4/C

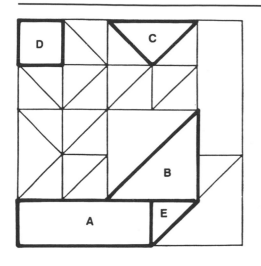

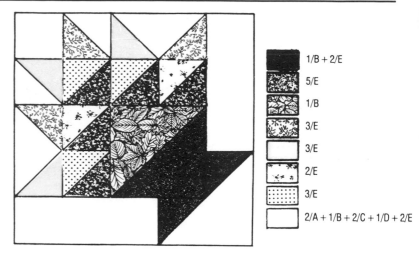

	1/B + 2/E
	5/E
	1/B
	3/E
	3/E
	2/E
	3/E
	2/A + 1/B + 2/C + 1/D + 2/E

TEMPLATE NUMBERS

	10" block	12" block	14" block
A	110	112	113
B	80	72	86
C	66	77	158
D	7	131	10
E	64	75	66

46
"May Basket"

INTERMEDIATE

BUILDING THE BLOCK

VARIATIONS

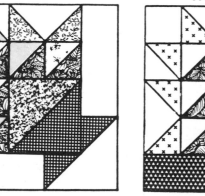

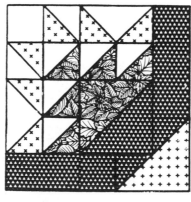

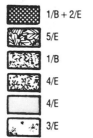

	1/B + 2/E
	5/E
	1/B
	4/E
	4/E
	3/E
	2/A + 1/B + 2/C + 1/D + 2/E

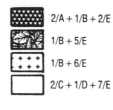

	2/A + 1/B + 2/E
	1/B + 5/E
	1/B + 6/E
	2/C + 1/D + 7/E

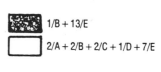

| | 1/B + 13/E |
| | 2/A + 2/B + 2/C + 1/D + 7/E |

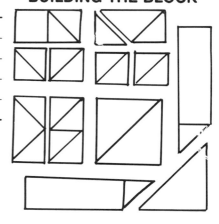

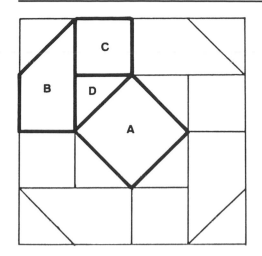

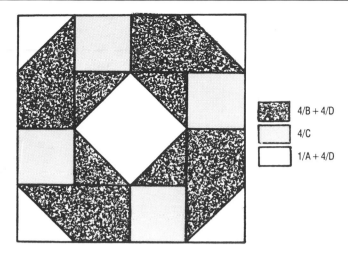

	4/B + 4/D
	4/C
	1/A + 4/D

47 "Big Foot"

INTERMEDIATE

TEMPLATE NUMBERS

	10" block	12" block	14" block
A	34	14	16
B	168	169	170
C	41	43	12
D	156	67	157

BUILDING THE BLOCK

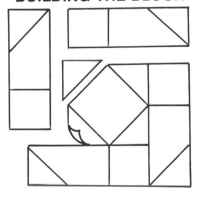

VARIATIONS

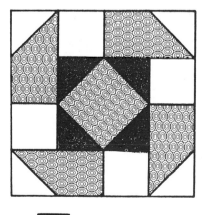

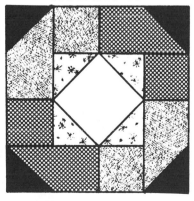

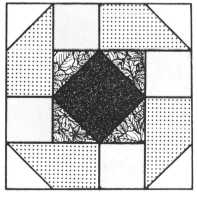

	4/D
	1/A + 4/B
	4/C + 4/D

	4/D
	2/B
	2/B + 4/C
	4/D
	1/A

	1/A
	4/D
	4/C
	4/B
	4/D

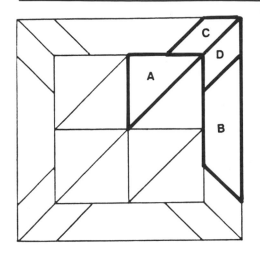

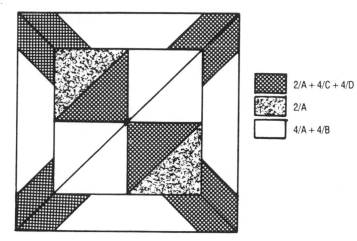

		2/A + 4/C + 4/D
		2/A
		4/A + 4/B

48
"Butterfly Bush"

INTERMEDIATE

TEMPLATE NUMBERS

	10" block	12" block	14" block
A	68	70	83
B	186	188	190
C	198	199	200
D	59	60	61

BUILDING THE BLOCK

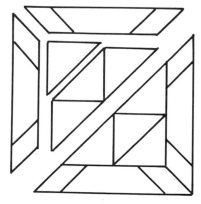

VARIATIONS

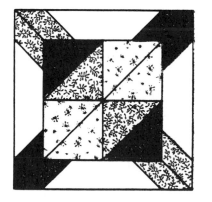

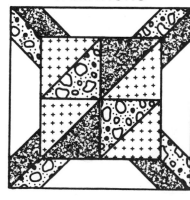

		2/A + 2/C + 2/D
		2/A + 2/C + 2/D
		4/A
		4/B

		2/A + 4/D
		2/A + 4/C
		4/A
		4/B

		4/A + 2/C + 2/D
		4/A + 2/C + 2/D
		4/B

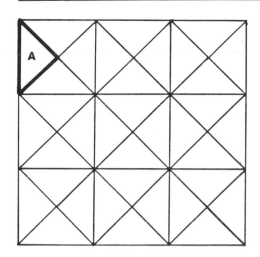

<table>
<tbody>
<tr><td>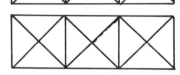</td></tr>
</tbody>
</table>

9/A
9/A
9/A
9/A

49 "Old Tippecanoe"

INTERMEDIATE

TEMPLATE NUMBERS

	10" block	12" block	14" block
A	65	76	68

BUILDING THE BLOCK

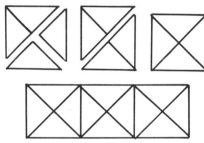

VARIATIONS

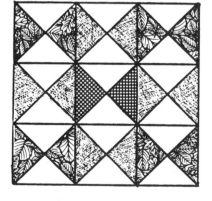

 2/A
8/A
8/A
18/A

 18/A
18/A

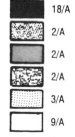 18/A
2/A
2/A
2/A
3/A
9/A

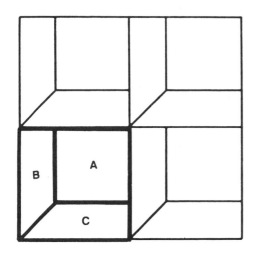

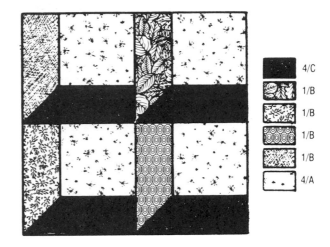

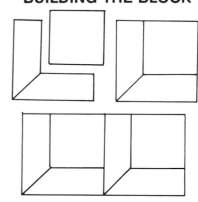

	4/C
	1/B
	1/B
	1/B
	1/B
	4/A

50
"Attic Windows"

INTERMEDIATE

TEMPLATE NUMBERS

	10" block	12" block	14" block
A	44	13	47
B	144	145	146
C	150	151	152

BUILDING THE BLOCK

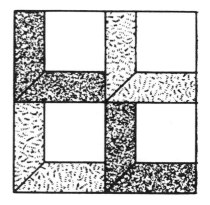

VARIATIONS

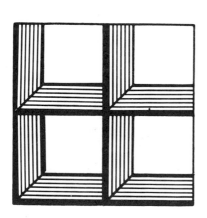

| | 4/B + 4/C |
| | 4/A |

	4/A
	4/C
	4/B

	2/B + 2/C
	2/B + 2/C
	4/A

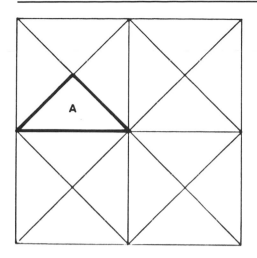

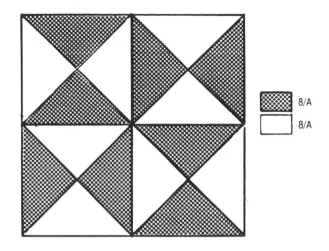

 8/A

 8/A

BUILDING THE BLOCK

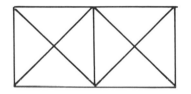

51
"Hour Glass"

INTERMEDIATE

TEMPLATE NUMBERS

	10" block	12" block	14" block
A	69	71	84

VARIATIONS

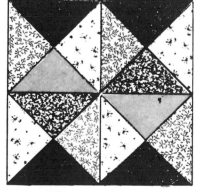

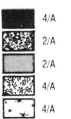 4/A
2/A
2/A
4/A
4/A

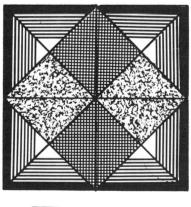

 4/A
8/A
4/A

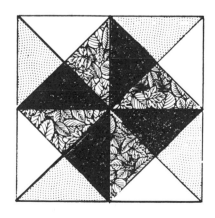

 4/A
4/A
4/A
4/A

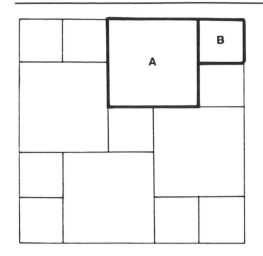

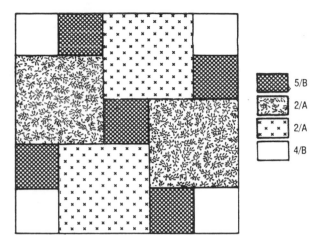

	5/B
	2/A
	2/A
	4/B

52
"Blocks & Dots"

INTERMEDIATE

TEMPLATE NUMBERS

	10" block	12" block	14" block
A	13	15	17
B	7	131	10

BUILDING THE BLOCK

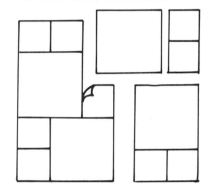

VARIATIONS

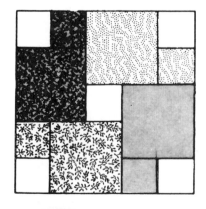

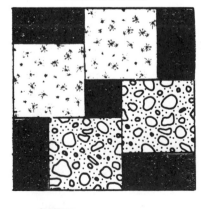

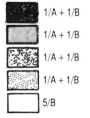

	1/A + 1/B
	1/A + 1/B
	1/A + 1/B
	1/A + 1/B
	5/B

	9/B
	2/A
	2/A

	2/A + 1/B
	2/A + 4/B
	4/B

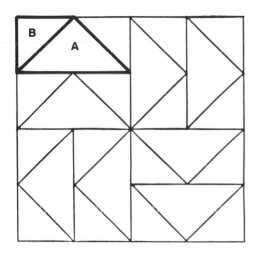

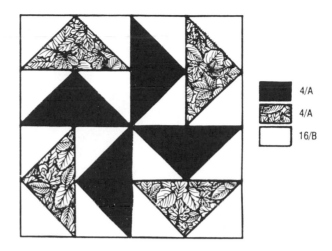

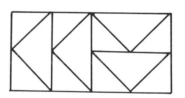

- 4/A
- 4/A
- 16/B

53 "Dutchman's Puzzle"

INTERMEDIATE

TEMPLATE NUMBERS

	10" block	12" block	14" block
A	69	71	84
B	156	67	157

BUILDING THE BLOCK

VARIATIONS

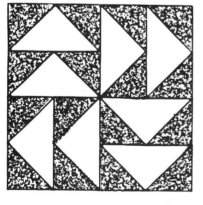

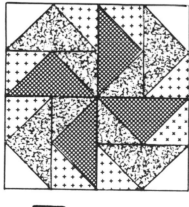

- 16/B
- 8/A

- 4/A
- 4/A
- 8/B
- 8/B

- 4/A
- 12/B
- 4/A
- 4/B

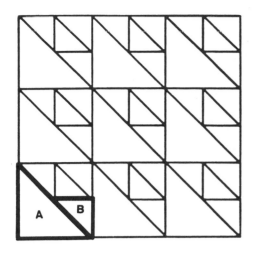

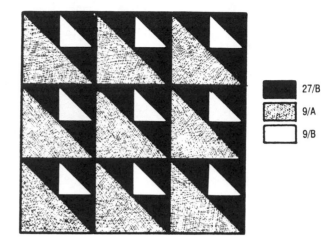

27/B

9/A

9/B

54
"Moon Race"

INTERMEDIATE

TEMPLATE NUMBERS

	10" block	12" block	14" block
A	68	70	83
B	63	154	155

BUILDING THE BLOCK

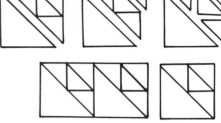

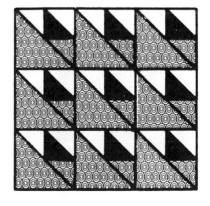

VARIATIONS

9/A + 9/B

27/B

7/A + 4/B

17/B

2/A + 15/B

9/B

9/A + 9/B

18/B

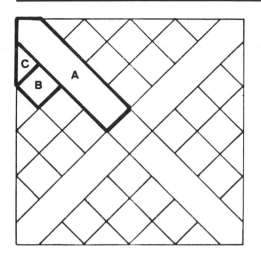

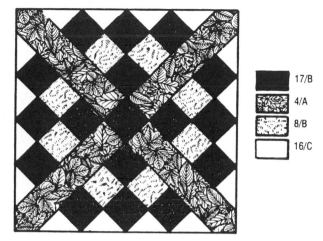

	17/B
	4/A
	8/B
	16/C

55 "Friendship"

INTERMEDIATE

TEMPLATE NUMBERS

	10" block	12" block	14" block
A	48	49	50
B	5	38	39
C	62	73	64

BUILDING THE BLOCK

VARIATIONS

	17/B + 16/C
	4/A + 8/B

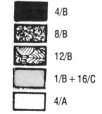
	4/B
	8/B
	12/B
	1/B + 16/C
	4/A

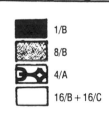
	1/B
	8/B
	4/A
	16/B + 16/C

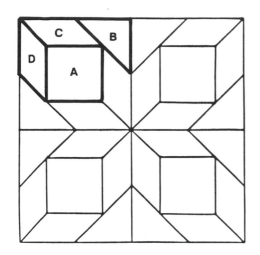

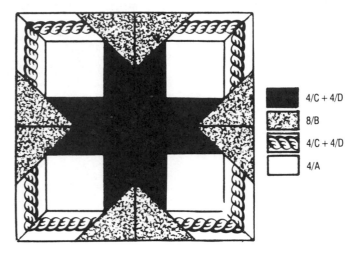

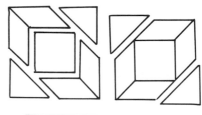

	4/C + 4/D
	8/B
	4/C + 4/D
	4/A

BUILDING THE BLOCK

TEMPLATE NUMBERS

	10"\nblock	12"\nblock	14"\nblock
A	41	43	12
B	156	67	157
C	1	2	3
D	122	123	125

56
"This 'n' That"

INTERMEDIATE

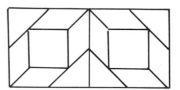

VARIATIONS

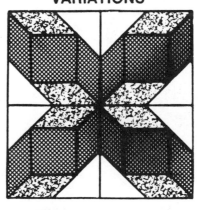

	4/C + 4/D
	4/C + 4/D
	8/B
	4/A

	4/A + 4/C + 4/D
	4/C + 4/D
	8/B

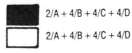

| | 2/A + 4/B + 4/C + 4/D |
| | 2/A + 4/B + 4/C + 4/D |

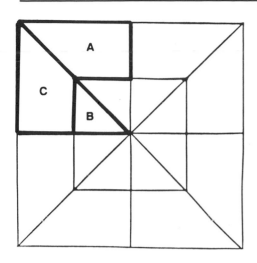

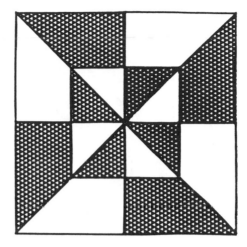

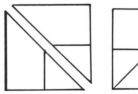

4/A + 4/B

4/B + 4/C

TEMPLATE NUMBERS

	10″ block	12″ block	14″ block
A	168	169	170
B	156	67	157
C	213	214	215

57
"Double Windmill"

INTERMEDIATE

BUILDING THE BLOCK

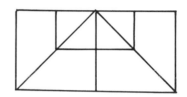

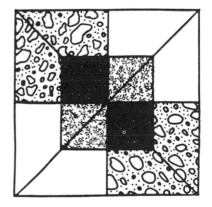

VARIATIONS

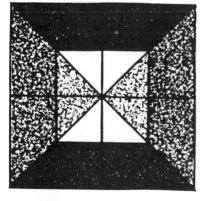

2/A + 2/C

2/A + 2/C

4/B

4/B

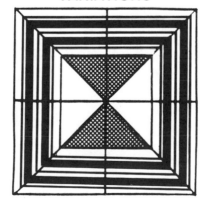

4/B

4/A + 4/C

4/B

4/B

4/B

2/A + 2/C

2/A + 2/C

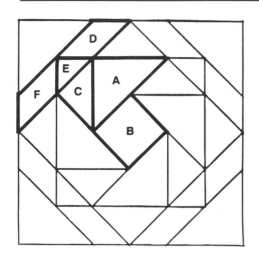

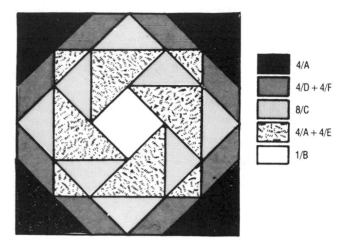

	4/A
	4/D + 4/F
	8/C
	4/A + 4/E
	1/B

58 "Vortex"

INTERMEDIATE

TEMPLATE NUMBERS

	10" block	12" block	14" block
A	68	70	83
B	33	42	11
C	65	76	68
D	198	199	200
E	63	154	155
F	59	60	61

BUILDING THE BLOCK

VARIATIONS

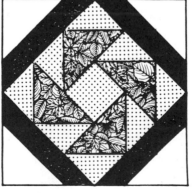

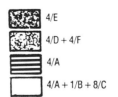

	4/E
	4/D + 4/F
	4/A
	4/A + 1/B + 8/C

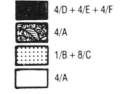

	4/D + 4/E + 4/F
	4/A
	1/B + 8/C
	4/A

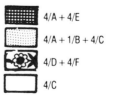

	4/A + 4/E
	4/A + 1/B + 4/C
	4/D + 4/F
	4/C

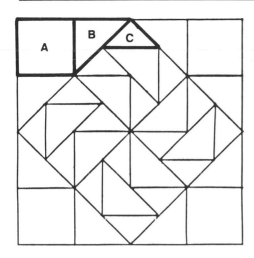

12/B

4/A + 4/B

16/C

59 "Martha's Whirl"

INTERMEDIATE

TEMPLATE NUMBERS

	10" block	12" block	14" block
A	41	43	12
B	156	67	157
C	153	74	75

BUILDING THE BLOCK

VARIATIONS

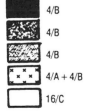

4/B

4/B

4/B

4/A + 4/B

16/C

8/B

8/B

4/A

16/C

4/A + 8/B

8/B + 16/C

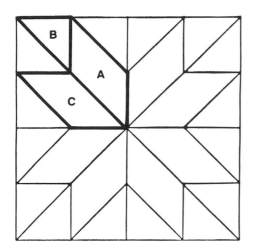

8/B + 4/C

4/A + 8/B

60 "Blazing Arrows"

INTERMEDIATE

TEMPLATE NUMBERS

	10" block	12" block	14" block
A	201	202	203
B	156	67	157
C	162	163	164

BUILDING THE BLOCK

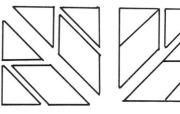

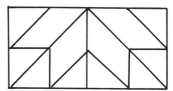

VARIATIONS

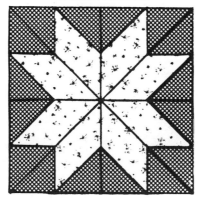

2/A + 2/C

8/B

8/B

2/A + 2/C

16/B

4/A + 4/C

8/B

4/A + 4/C

8/B

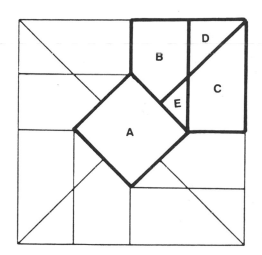

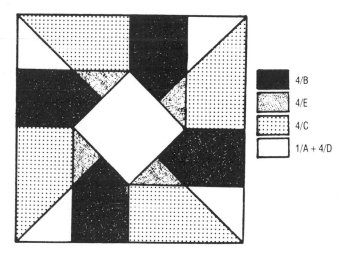

		4/B
		4/E
		4/C
		1/A + 4/D

61 "Country Homes"

INTERMEDIATE

TEMPLATE NUMBERS

	10" block	12" block	14" block
A	34	14	16
B	132	133	134
C	168	169	170
D	156	67	157
E	153	74	75

BUILDING THE BLOCK

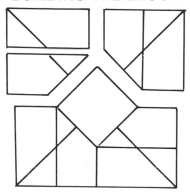

VARIATIONS

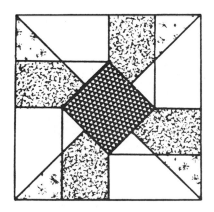

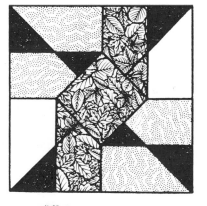

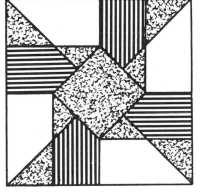

	1/A
	4/B
	4/D
	4/C + 4/E

	4/D + 2/E
	1/A + 2/B + 2/E
	2/B + 2/C
	2/C

	1/A + 4/D + 4/E
	4/B
	4/C

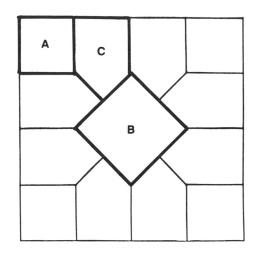

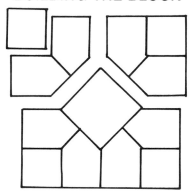

4/A

8/C

1/B

62 "Susannah Patch"

INTERMEDIATE

TEMPLATE NUMBERS

	10" block	12" block	14" block
A	41	43	12
B	34	14	16
C	132	133	134

BUILDING THE BLOCK

VARIATIONS

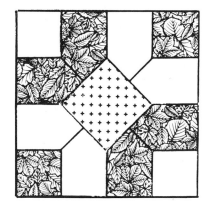

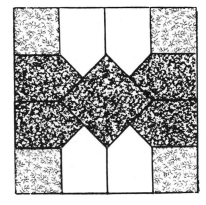

2/A + 4/C

1/B

2/A + 4/C

1/B + 4/C

4/A

4/C

1/B + 4/C

4/A

4/C

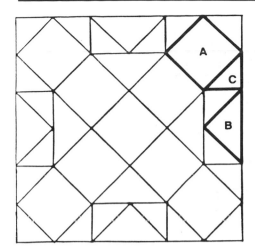

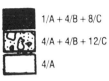

1/A + 4/B + 8/C
4/A + 4/B + 12/C
4/A

63 "Swing in the Center"

INTERMEDIATE

TEMPLATE NUMBERS

	10" block	12" block	14" block
A	33	42	11
B	65	76	68
C	63	154	155

BUILDING THE BLOCK

VARIATIONS

8/A + 8/C
1/A + 8/B + 12/C

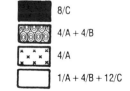

8/C
4/A + 4/B
4/A
1/A + 4/B + 12/C

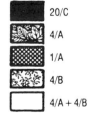

20/C
4/A
1/A
4/B
4/A + 4/B

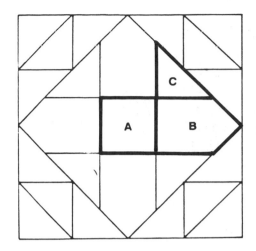

1/A + 8/C

4/B

12/C

64
"Li'l Bit"

INTERMEDIATE

	TEMPLATE NUMBERS		
	10" block	12" block	14" block
A	41	43	12
B	132	133	134
C	156	67	157

BUILDING THE BLOCK

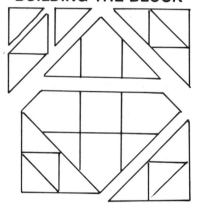

VARIATIONS

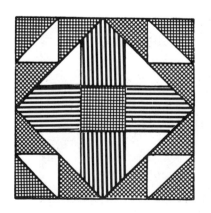

1/A + 12/C

4/B

8/C

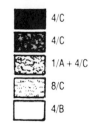

4/C

4/C

1/A + 4/C

8/C

4/B

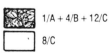

1/A + 4/B + 12/C

8/C

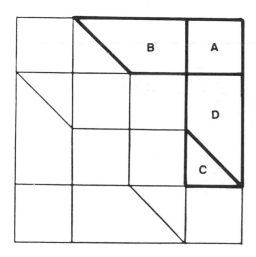

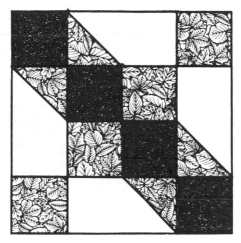

	4/A
	4/A + 4/C
	2/B + 2/D

65 "Road to Oklahoma"

INTERMEDIATE

TEMPLATE NUMBERS

	10" block	12" block	14" block
A	41	43	12
B	168	169	170
C	156	67	157
D	213	214	215

BUILDING THE BLOCK

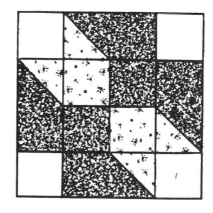

VARIATIONS

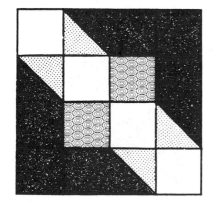

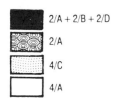

	2/A + 2/B + 2/D
	2/A
	4/C
	4/A

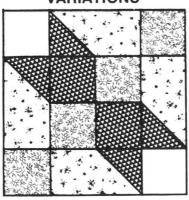

	2/A + 4/C
	4/A
	2/B + 2/D
	2/A

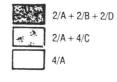

	2/A + 2/B + 2/D
	2/A + 4/C
	4/A

119

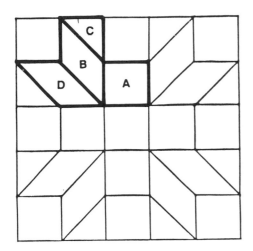

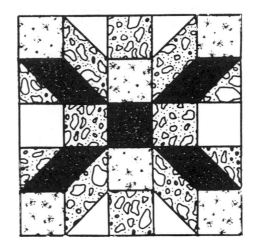

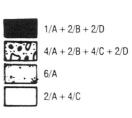

■	1/A + 2/B + 2/D
▨	4/A + 2/B + 4/C + 2/D
▫	6/A
☐	2/A + 4/C

66 "Miller's Daughter"

INTERMEDIATE

TEMPLATE NUMBERS

	10" block	12" block	14" block
A	7	131	10
B	101	102	103
C	64	75	66
D	177	178	179

BUILDING THE BLOCK

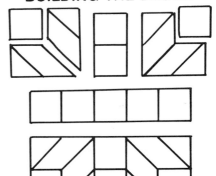

VARIATIONS

■	8/A + 8/C
▥	4/A + 4/B + 4/D
☐	1/A

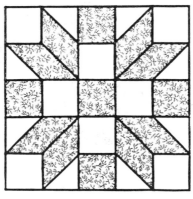

▨	5/A + 4/B + 4/D
☐	8/A + 8/C

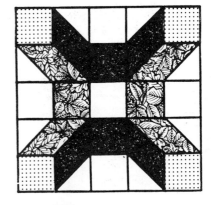

■	2/A + 2/B + 2/D
▨	2/A + 2/B + 2/D
▫	4/A
☐	5/A + 8/C

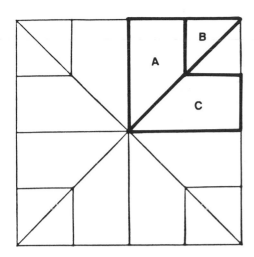

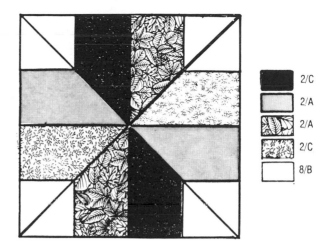

	2/C
	2/A
	2/A
	2/C
	8/B

67
"End of Day"

INTERMEDIATE

TEMPLATE NUMBERS

	10" block	12" block	14" block
A	168	169	170
B	156	67	157
C	213	214	215

BUILDING THE BLOCK

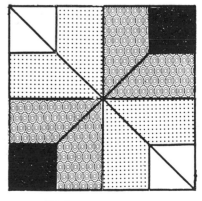

VARIATIONS

 8/B
4/A + 4/C

 4/B + 4/C
4/A + 4/B

4/B
2/A + 2/C
2/A + 2/C
4/B

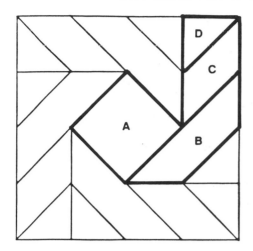

2/B + 2/C

1/A + 8/D

2/B + 2/C

68
"Symmetry in Motion"

INTERMEDIATE

TEMPLATE NUMBERS

	10" block	12" block	14" block
A	34	14	16
B	187	189	191
C	162	163	164
D	156	67	157

BUILDING THE BLOCK

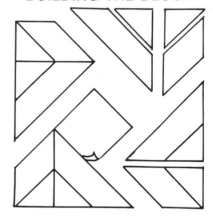

VARIATIONS

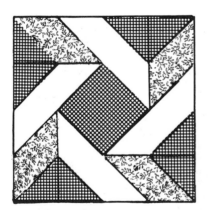

1/A + 8/D

4/C

4/B

4/D

4/D

1/A

4/B + 4/C

4/B + 4/D

1/A + 4/C + 4/D

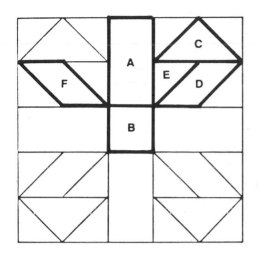

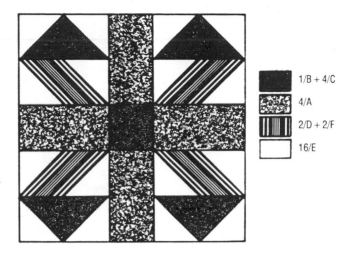

▨	1/B + 4/C
░	4/A
▥	2/D + 2/F
□	16/E

69
"Helen's Folly"

INTERMEDIATE

TEMPLATE NUMBERS

	10" block	12" block	14" block
A	90	91	56
B	7	131	10
C	66	77	158
D	101	102	103
E	64	75	66
F	177	178	179

BUILDING THE BLOCK

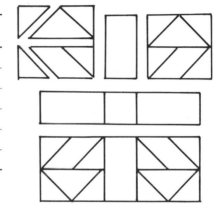

VARIATIONS

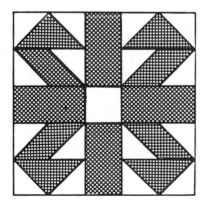

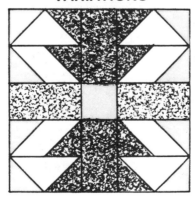

▨	4/A + 4/C + 2/D + 2/F
□	1/B + 16/E

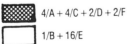

░	2/A + 8/E
░	2/A
▨	1/B + 8/E
□	4/C + 2/D + 2/F

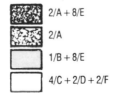

▨	4/A + 1/B
🍃	4/C + 2/D + 2/F
□	16/E

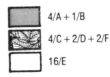

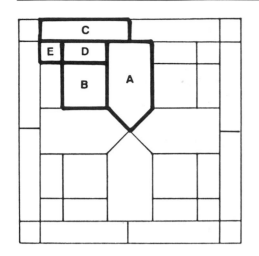

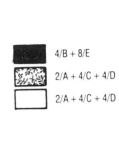

4/B + 8/E

2/A + 4/C + 4/D

2/A + 4/C + 4/D

70 "Dignity"

INTERMEDIATE

TEMPLATE NUMBERS

	10" block	12" block	14" block
A	128	129	130
B	7	131	10
C	114	18	116
D	51	52	53
E	35	4	31

BUILDING THE BLOCK

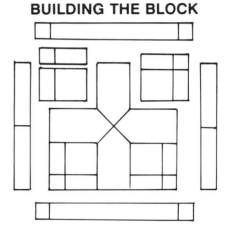

VARIATIONS

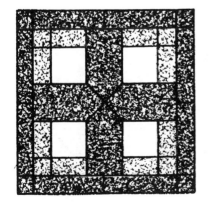

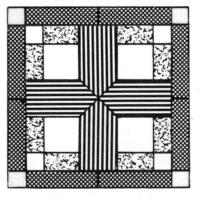

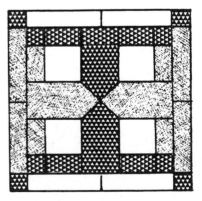

4/A + 8/C + 4/E

8/D + 4/E

4/B

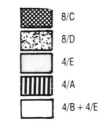

8/C

8/D

4/E

4/A

4/B + 4/E

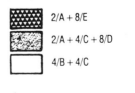

2/A + 8/E

2/A + 4/C + 8/D

4/B + 4/C

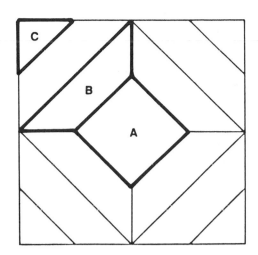

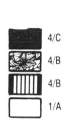

	4/C
	4/B
	4/B
	1/A

71
"Mosaic"

INTERMEDIATE

TEMPLATE NUMBERS

	10" block	12" block	14" block
A	34	14	16
B	187	189	191
C	156	67	157

BUILDING THE BLOCK

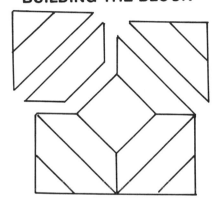

VARIATIONS

	4/B + 4/C
	1/A + 4/B

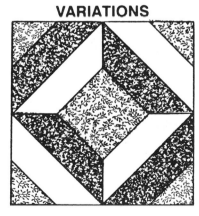

	4/B
	1/A + 4/C
	4/B

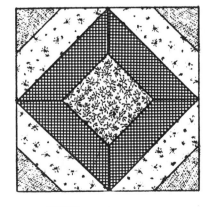

	4/B
	1/A
	4/C
	4/B

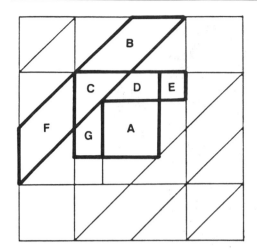

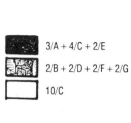

3/A + 4/C + 2/E

2/B + 2/D + 2/F + 2/G

10/C

TEMPLATE NUMBERS

	10" block	12" block	14" block
A	41	43	12
B	201	202	203
C	156	67	157
D	195	196	197
E	36	37	32
F	162	163	164
G	28	29	30

72
"Mohawk"

INTERMEDIATE

BUILDING THE BLOCK

VARIATIONS

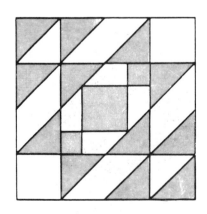

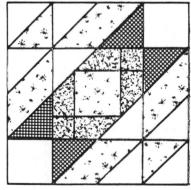

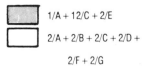
1/A + 12/C + 2/E

2/A + 2/B + 2/C + 2/D +
2/F + 2/G

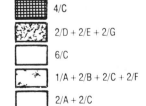
4/C

2/D + 2/E + 2/G

6/C

1/A + 2/B + 2/C + 2/F

2/A + 2/C

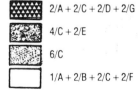
2/A + 2/C + 2/D + 2/G

4/C + 2/E

6/C

1/A + 2/B + 2/C + 2/F

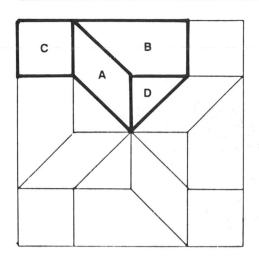

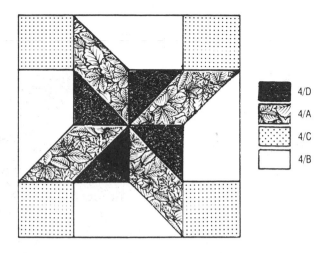

		4/D
		4/A
		4/C
		4/B

73
"Clay's Choice"

INTERMEDIATE

TEMPLATE NUMBERS

	10" block	12" block	14" block
A	201	202	203
B	168	169	170
C	41	43	12
D	156	67	157

BUILDING THE BLOCK

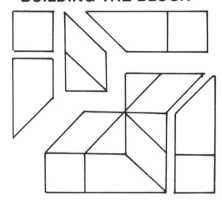

VARIATIONS

	4/B + 4/C
	4/A
	4/D

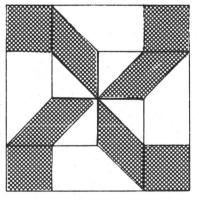

	4/A + 4/C
	4/B + 4/D

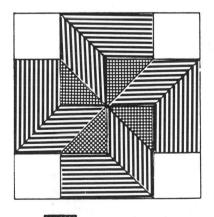

	4/D
	4/A + 4/B
	4/C

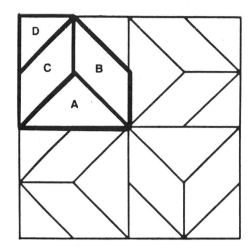

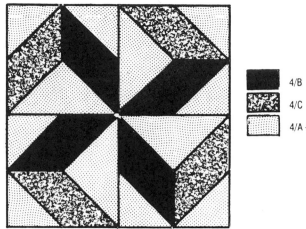

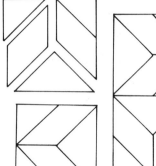

4/B

4/C

4/A + 8/D

74 "Flyfoot"

INTERMEDIATE

TEMPLATE NUMBERS

	10" block	12" block	14" block
A	69	71	84
B	201	202	203
C	162	163	164
D	156	67	157

BUILDING THE BLOCK

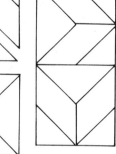

VARIATIONS

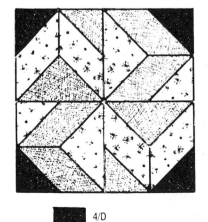

4/D

2/A + 2/B + 2/C + 2/D

2/A + 2/B + 2/C + 2/D

4/A + 8/D

4/B + 4/C

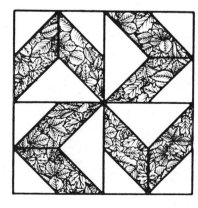

4/B + 4/C

4/A + 8/D

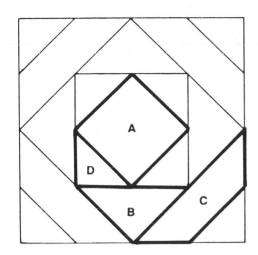

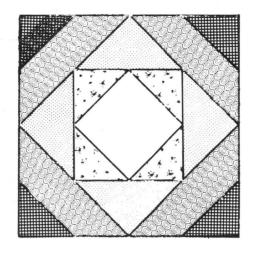

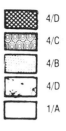

	4/D
	4/C
	4/B
	4/D
	1/A

75
"Peace"

INTERMEDIATE

TEMPLATE NUMBERS

	10" block	12" block	14" block
A	34	14	16
B	69	71	84
C	187	189	191
D	156	67	157

BUILDING THE BLOCK

VARIATIONS

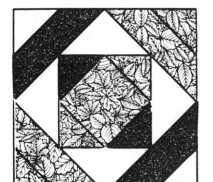

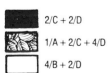

	2/C + 2/D
	1/A + 2/C + 4/D
	4/B + 2/D

	4/B
	4/C + 4/D
	4/D
	1/A

| | 1/A + 4/B + 4/D |
| | 4/C + 4/D |

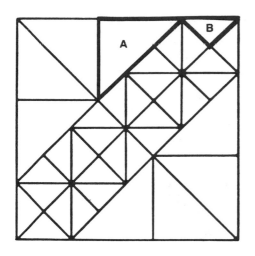

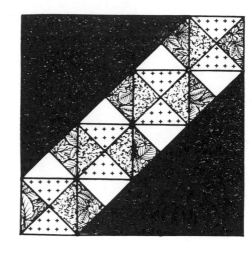

	8/A
	8/B
	6/B
	8/B
	6/B

76
"Starry Paths"

INTERMEDIATE

TEMPLATE NUMBERS			
	10" block	12" block	14" block
A	79	82	85
B	153	74	75

BUILDING THE BLOCK

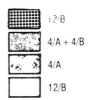

VARIATIONS

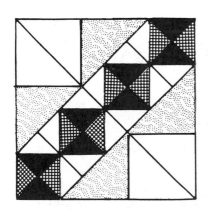

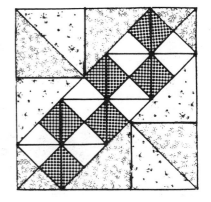

	8/B
	8/B
	4/A
	4/A + 12/B

	12/B
	4/A + 4/B
	4/A
	12/B

	12/B
	4/A + 4/B
	4/A
	12/B

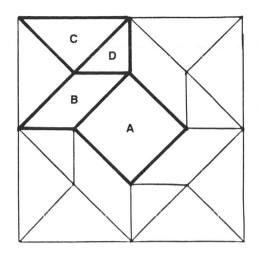

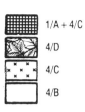

	1/A + 4/C
	4/D
	4/C
	4/B

77 "Windblown Star"

INTERMEDIATE

TEMPLATE NUMBERS

	10" block	12" block	14" block
A	34	14	16
B	201	202	203
C	69	71	84
D	156	67	157

BUILDING THE BLOCK

VARIATIONS

	2/B
	1/A + 4/C
	2/B + 4/C
	4/D

	4/B + 4/C
	1/A + 4/C + 4/D

	4/D
	4/B
	8/C
	1/A

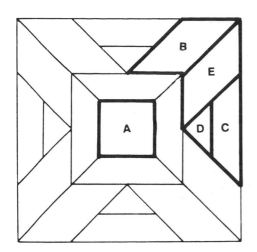

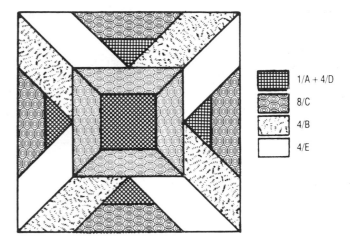

	1/A + 4/D
	8/C
	4/B
	4/E

TEMPLATE NUMBERS

	10" block	12" block	14" block
A	41	43	12
B	201	202	203
C	180	182	184
D	153	74	75
E	162	163	164

78
"Star Wars"

INTERMEDIATE

BUILDING THE BLOCK

VARIATIONS

	1/A + 4/D
	4/C
	4/B + 4/C + 4/E

	4/C + 4D
	4/B + 4/E
	1/A + 4/C

	2/B + 4/C + 2/E
	2/B + 4/D + 2/E
	1/A
	4/C

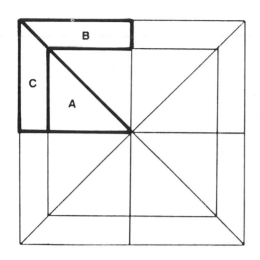

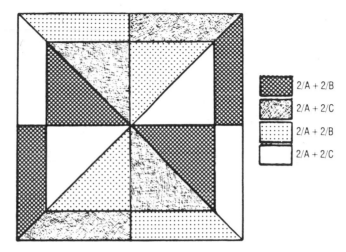

		2/A + 2/B	
		2/A + 2/C	
		2/A + 2/B	
		2/A + 2/C	

79
"Stroll Around the Block"

INTERMEDIATE

TEMPLATE NUMBERS

	10" block	12" block	14" block
A	69	71	84
B	204	205	206
C	20	21	22

BUILDING THE BLOCK

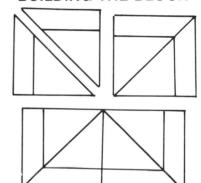

VARIATIONS

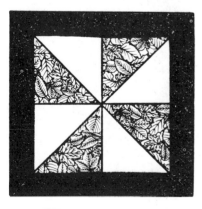

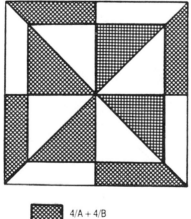

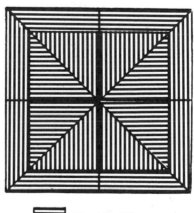

	4/B + 4/C
	4/A
	4/A

	4/A + 4/B
	4/A + 4/C

	8/A + 4/B + 4/C

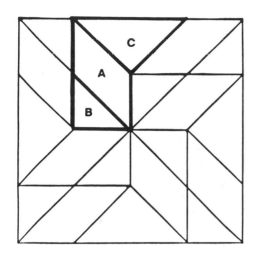

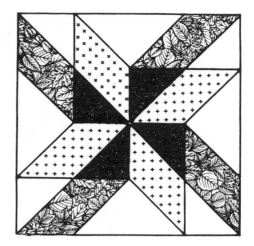

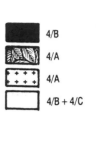

	4/B
	4/A
	4/A
	4/B + 4/C

80
"Old Poinsettia"

INTERMEDIATE

TEMPLATE NUMBERS

	10" block	12" block	14" block
A	69	71	84
B	201	202	203
C	156	·67	157

BUILDING THE BLOCK

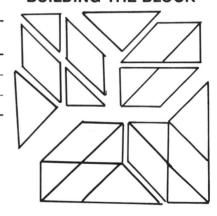

VARIATIONS

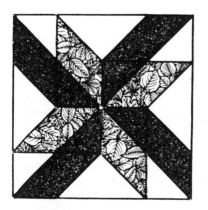

	4/A + 4/B
	4/A
	4/B + 4/C

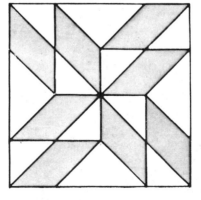

	8/A
	4/B + 4/C

	4/B + 4/C
	2/A + 2/B
	2/A + 2/B
	4/A

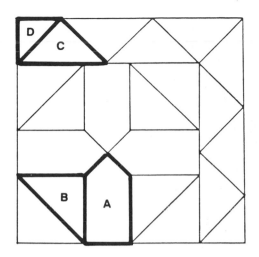

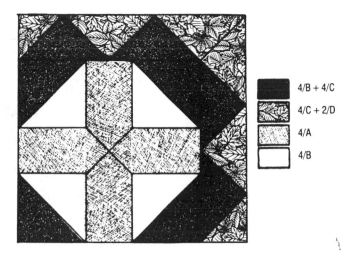

	4/B + 4/C
	4/C + 2/D
	4/A
	4/B

81
"Off-Beat"

INTERMEDIATE

TEMPLATE NUMBERS

	10" block	12" block	14" block
A	128	129	130
B	67	78	81
C	66	77	158
D	64	75	66

BUILDING THE BLOCK

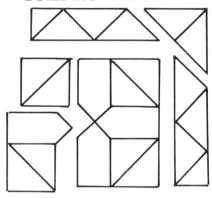

VARIATIONS

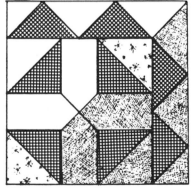

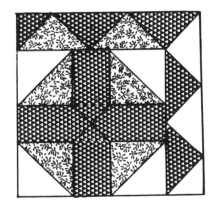

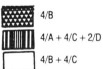

	4/B
	4/A + 4/C + 2/D
	4/B + 4/C

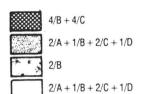

	4/B + 4/C
	2/A + 1/B + 2/C + 1/D
	2/B
	2/A + 1/B + 2/C + 1/D

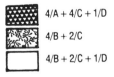

	4/A + 4/C + 1/D
	4/B + 2/C
	4/B + 2/C + 1/D

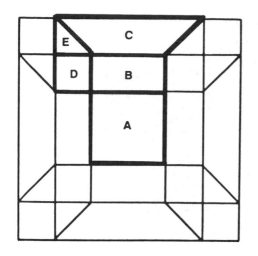

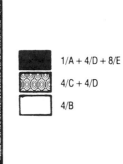

1/A + 4/D + 8/E

4/C + 4/D

4/B

82
"Water Fins"

INTERMEDIATE

TEMPLATE NUMBERS

	10" block	12" block	14" block
A	44	13	47
B	23	24	25
C	186	188	190
D	6	39	40
E	63	154	155

BUILDING THE BLOCK

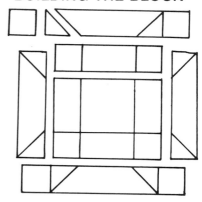

VARIATIONS

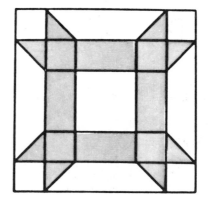

1/A + 8/D

4/C

4/B + 8/E

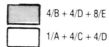

4/B + 4/D + 8/E

1/A + 4/C + 4/D

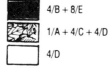

4/B + 8/E

1/A + 4/C + 4/D

4/D

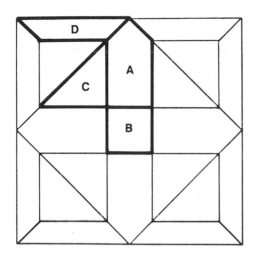

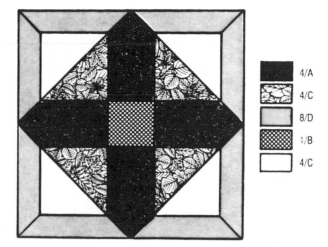

■	4/A
(leaf)	4/C
(gray)	8/D
(grid)	1/B
□	4/C

83 "Picnic"

INTERMEDIATE

TEMPLATE NUMBERS

	10" block	12" block	14" block
A	128	129	130
B	7	131	10
C	67	78	81
D	192	193	194

BUILDING THE BLOCK

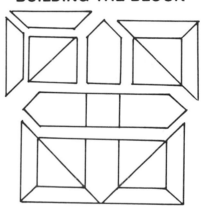

VARIATIONS

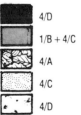

■	4/D
(gray)	1/B + 4/C
(leaf)	4/A
(dots)	4/C
(speckle)	4/D

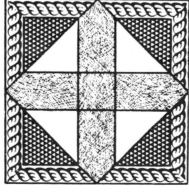

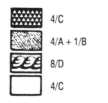

(triangles)	4/C
(lines)	4/A + 1/B
(rope)	8/D
□	4/C

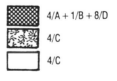

(grid)	4/A + 1/B + 8/D
(floral)	4/C
□	4/C

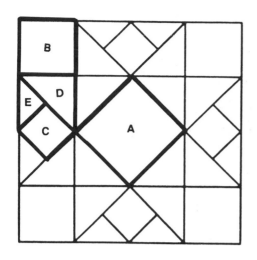

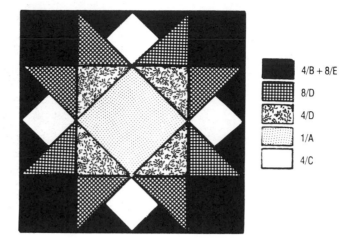

				4/B + 8/E
				8/D
				4/D
				1/A
				4/C

84
"Royalty"

INTERMEDIATE

TEMPLATE NUMBERS

	10" block	12" block	14" block
A	34	14	16
B	41	43	12
C	32	8	9
D	156	67	157
E	153	74	75

BUILDING THE BLOCK

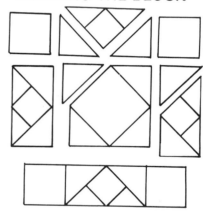

VARIATIONS

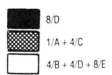

8/D

1/A + 4/C

4/B + 4/D + 8/E

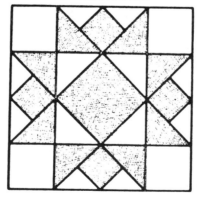

1/A + 4/C + 8/D

4/B + 4/D + 8/E

4/C

12/D

1/A

4/B + 8/E

138

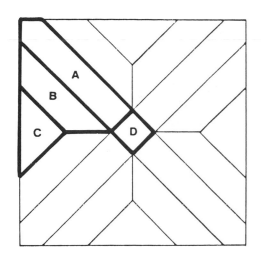

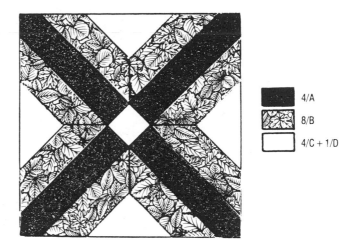

	4/A
	8/B
	4/C + 1/D

85
"Carol's Cross"

INTERMEDIATE

TEMPLATE NUMBERS

	10" block	12" block	14" block
A	48	49	50
B	181	183	185
C	66	77	158
D	5	38	39

BUILDING THE BLOCK

VARIATIONS

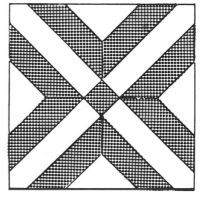

	4/A
	4/C + 1/D
	8/B

	2/C
	4/B
	4/B + 1/D
	4/A + 2/C

| | 8/B + 1/D |
| | 4/A + 4/C |

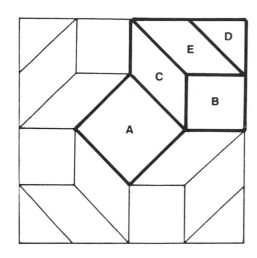

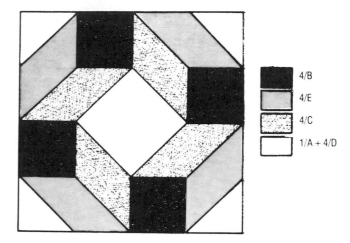

	4/B
	4/E
	4/C
	1/A + 4/D

86 "Bachelor's Puzzle"

ADVANCED

TEMPLATE NUMBERS

	10" block	12" block	14" block
A	34	14	16
B	41	43	12
C	201	202	203
D	156	67	157
E	162	163	164

BUILDING THE BLOCK

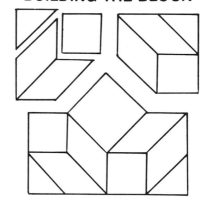

VARIATIONS

	4/B
	4/C + 4/E
	1/A + 4/D

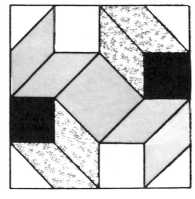

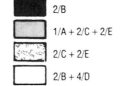

	2/B
	1/A + 2/C + 2/E
	2/C + 2/E
	2/B + 4/D

	4/C
	4/E
	1/A
	4/B + 4/D

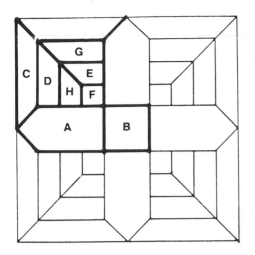

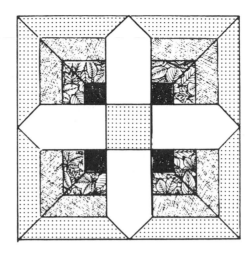

4/F

4/E + 4/H

4/D + 4/G

1/B + 8/C

4/A

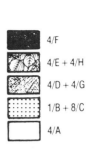

87 "Perception"

ADVANCED

TEMPLATE NUMBERS

	10" block	12" block	14" block
A	128	129	130
B	7	131	10
C	192	193	194
D	147	148	149
E	141	142	143
F	35	4	31
G	135	136	137
H	207	208	209

BUILDING THE BLOCK

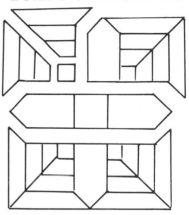

VARIATIONS

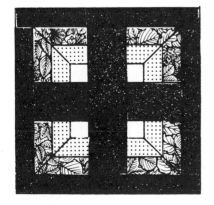

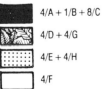

4/A + 1/B + 8/C

4/D + 4/G

4/E + 4/H

4/F

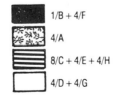

1/B + 4/F

4/A

8/C + 4/E + 4/H

4/D + 4/G

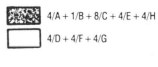

4/A + 1/B + 8/C + 4/E + 4/H

4/D + 4/F + 4/G

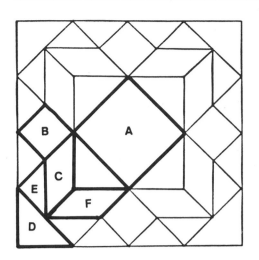

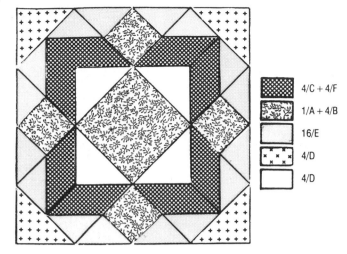

	4/C + 4/F
	1/A + 4/B
	16/E
	4/D
	4/D

88 "Farmer's Fields"

ADVANCED

TEMPLATE NUMBERS

	10" block	12" block	14" block
A	34	14	16
B	32	8	9
C	1	2	3
D	156	67	157
E	153	74	75
F	122	123	125

BUILDING THE BLOCK

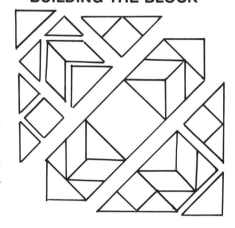

VARIATIONS

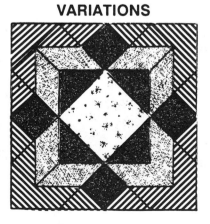

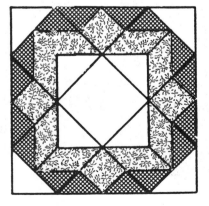

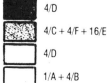

	4/D
	4/C + 4/F + 16/E
	4/D
	1/A + 4/B

	4/B + 4/D
	4/D + 16/E
	4/C + 4/F
	1/A

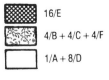

	16/E
	4/B + 4/C + 4/F
	1/A + 8/D

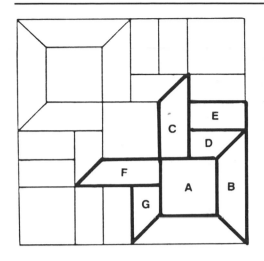

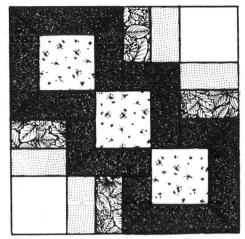

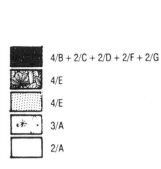

		4/B + 2/C + 2/D + 2/F + 2/G
		4/E
		4/E
		3/A
		2/A

TEMPLATE NUMBERS

	10" block	12" block	14" block
A	41	43	12
B	180	182	184
C	95	96	97
D	195	196	197
E	87	88	89
F	171	172	173
G	28	29	30

89
"Sizzlin'
Squares"

ADVANCED

BUILDING THE BLOCK

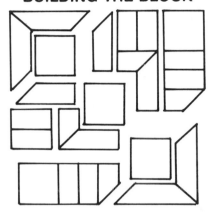

VARIATIONS

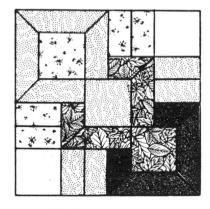

	2/B + 1/D + 1/G
	1/A + 1/C + 1/D + 1/F + 1/G
	1/A + 2/B + 1/C + 4/E + 1/F
	1/A + 4/E
	2/A

	4/E
	4/E
	1/C + 1/D + 1/F + 1/G
	2/B + 1/C + 1/F
	2/B + 1/D + 1/G
	2/A
	3/A

	5/A
	4/E
	4/E
	4/B + 2/C + 2/D + 2/F + 2/G

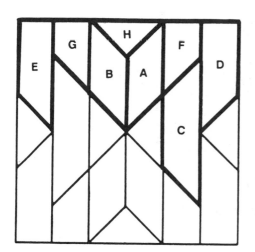

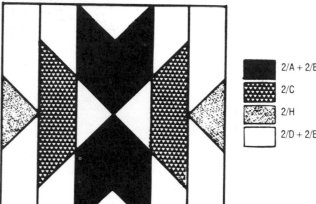

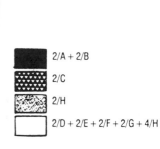

2/A + 2/B

2/C

2/H

2/D + 2/E + 2/F + 2/G + 4/H

90 "Squash Blossom"

ADVANCED

TEMPLATE NUMBERS

	10" block	12" block	14" block
A	219	220	221
B	124	126	127
C	186	188	190
D	144	145	146
E	150	151	152
F	165	166	167
G	210	211	212
H	65	76	68

BUILDING THE BLOCK

VARIATIONS

2/A + 2/B + 2/C + 2/H

2/D + 2/E + 2/F + 2/G + 4/H

4/H

2/A + 2/B + 2/C

2/D + 2/E + 2/F + 2/G + 2/H

6/H

2/F + 2/G

2/D + 2/E

2/A + 2/B + 2/C

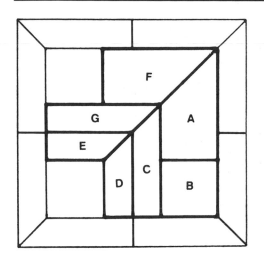

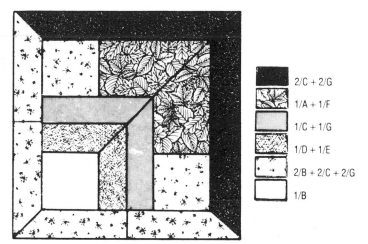

	2/C + 2/G
	1/A + 1/F
	1/C + 1/G
	1/D + 1/E
	2/B + 2/C + 2/G
	1/B

91
"Center Stage"

ADVANCED

TEMPLATE NUMBERS

	10" block	12" block	14" block
A	168	169	170
B	41	43	12
C	204	205	206
D	95	96	97
E	171	172	173
F	213	214	215
G	20	21	22

BUILDING THE BLOCK

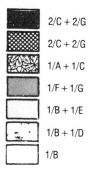

VARIATIONS

	3/C + 1/D + 1/E + 3/G
	1/B + 2/C + 2/G
	1/A + 1/F
	2/B

	5/C + 5/G
	1/A + 1/D + 1/E + 1/F
	2/B
	1/B

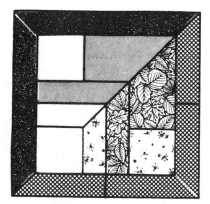

	2/C + 2/G
	2/C + 2/G
	1/A + 1/C
	1/F + 1/G
	1/B + 1/E
	1/B + 1/D
	1/B

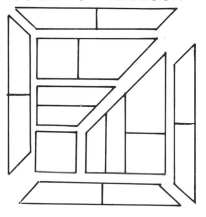

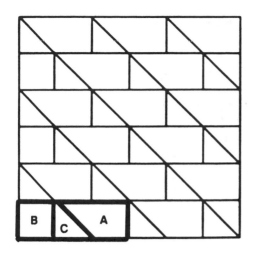

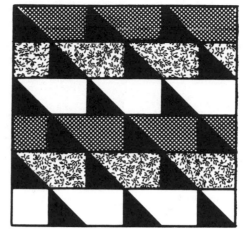

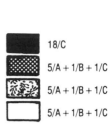

18/C

5/A + 1/B + 1/C

5/A + 1/B + 1/C

5/A + 1/B + 1/C

92
"Flight Formation"

ADVANCED

TEMPLATE NUMBERS			
	10" block	12" block	14" block
A	165	166	167
B	6	39	40
C	63	154	155

BUILDING THE BLOCK

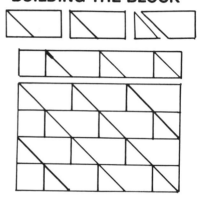

VARIATIONS

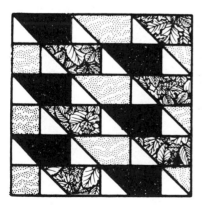

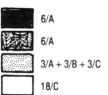

6/A

6/A

3/A + 3/B + 3/C

18/C

18/C

6/A + 3/B

9/A + 3/C

15/A + 3/B + 3/C

18/C

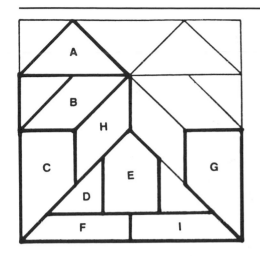

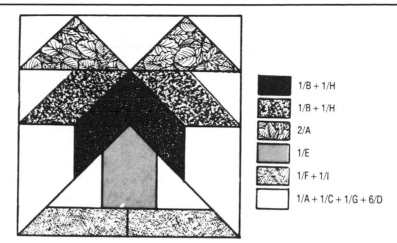

- ▮ 1/B + 1/H
- ▦ 1/B + 1/H
- ▨ 2/A
- ▧ 1/E
- ▨ 1/F + 1/I
- ☐ 1/A + 1/C + 1/G + 6/D

93
"Waving Palm"

ADVANCED

TEMPLATE NUMBERS

	10" block	12" block	14" block
A	69	71	84
B	201	202	203
C	168	169	170
D	156	67	157
E	132	133	134
F	20	21	22
G	213	214	215
H	162	163	164
I	204	205	206

BUILDING THE BLOCK

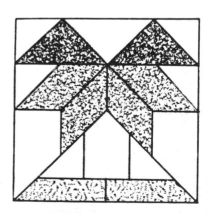

VARIATIONS

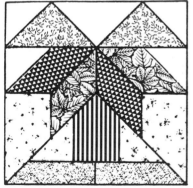

- ▨ 2/B
- ▤ 1/E
- ▨ 2/H
- ▨ 1/F + 1/I
- ▨ 2/A
- ▨ 1/C + 1/G + 2/D
- ☐ 1/A + 4/D

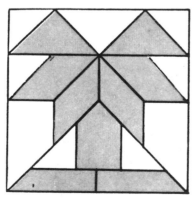

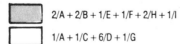

- ▨ 2/A + 2/B + 1/E + 1/F + 2/H + 1/I
- ☐ 1/A + 1/C + 6/D + 1/G

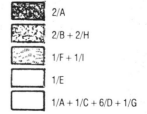

- ▮ 2/A
- ▨ 2/B + 2/H
- ▨ 1/F + 1/I
- ☐ 1/E
- ☐ 1/A + 1/C + 6/D + 1/G

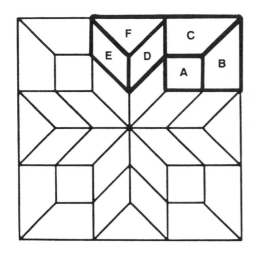

■		4/D + 4/E	
▢		4/B + 4/C + 4/F	
▨		4/D + 4/E	
□		4/A	

94
"Starbright"

___

ADVANCED

TEMPLATE NUMBERS

	10" block	12" block	14" block
A	6	39	40
B	165	166	167
C	210	211	212
D	59	60	61
E	198	199	200
F	65	76	68

BUILDING THE BLOCK

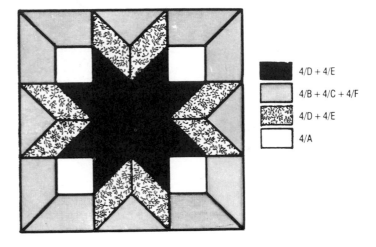

VARIATIONS

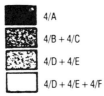

■	4/A
▨	4/B + 4/C
▨	4/D + 4/E
□	4/D + 4/E + 4/F

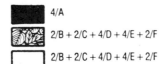

■	4/A
▨	2/B + 2/C + 4/D + 4/E + 2/F
□	2/B + 2/C + 4/D + 4/E + 2/F

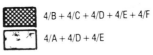

▨	4/B + 4/C + 4/D + 4/E + 4/F
□	4/A + 4/D + 4/E

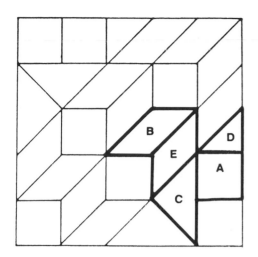

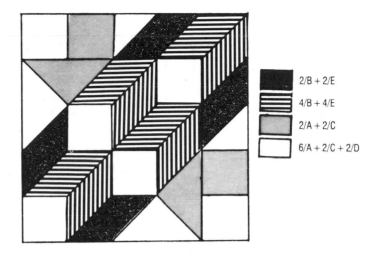

2/B + 2/E

4/B + 4/E

2/A + 2/C

6/A + 2/C + 2/D

95
"Arrows"

ADVANCED

TEMPLATE NUMBERS

	10" block	12" block	14" block
A	7	131	10
B	101	102	103
C	66	77	158
D	64	75	66
E	177	178	179

BUILDING THE BLOCK

VARIATIONS

1/D + 6/E

4/C

6/B + 1/D

8/A

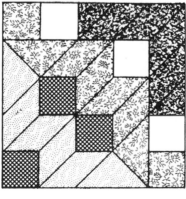

2/B + 2/D + 2/E

3/A

2/A + 2/B + 2/C + 2/E

2/B + 2/C + 2/E

3/A

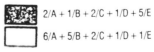

2/A + 1/B + 2/C + 1/D + 5/E

6/A + 5/B + 2/C + 1/D + 1/E

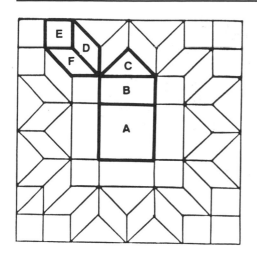

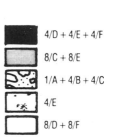

■	4/D + 4/E + 4/F
▨	8/C + 8/E
▨	1/A + 4/B + 4/C
▨	4/E
□	8/D + 8/F

**96
"Friendship
Star"**

___

ADVANCED

TEMPLATE NUMBERS

	10" block	12" block	14" block
A	41	43	12
B	87	88	89
C	153	74	75
D	98	99	100
E	36	37	32
F	174	175	176

BUILDING THE BLOCK

VARIATIONS

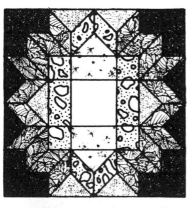

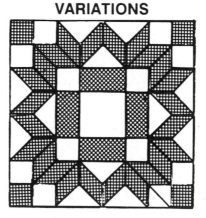

■	4/C + 12/E
▨	10/D + 10/F
▨	2/B + 2/D + 4/E + 2/F
▨	6/C
▨	2/B + 2/C
□	1/A

▨	4/B + 12/D + 4/E + 12/F
□	1/A + 12/C + 12/E

■	1/A + 12/C + 4/E
▨	4/D + 4/F
▤	4/D + 4/F
▨	4/E
▨	4/D + 4/F
□	4/B + 8/E

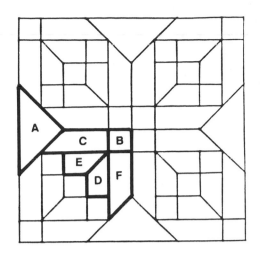

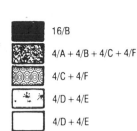

■	16/B
▨	4/A + 4/B + 4/C + 4/F
▦	4/C + 4/F
▨	4/D + 4/E
□	4/D + 4/E

BUILDING THE BLOCK

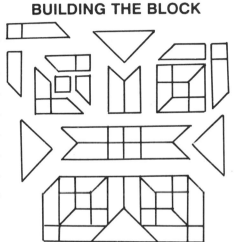

97 "Old-Fashioned Daisy"

___

ADVANCED

TEMPLATE NUMBERS

	10″ block	12″ block	14″ block
A	66	77	158
B	35	4	31
C	147	148	149
D	141	142	143
E	207	208	209
F	135	136	137

VARIATIONS

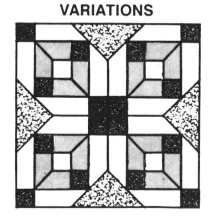

	4/A + 16/B + 8/D + 8/E
□	4/B + 8/C + 8/F

■	16/B
▨	8/D + 8/E
▦	4/A
□	4/B + 8/C + 8/F

■	8/B + 8/C + 8/F
	4/A + 4/D + 4/E
□	12/B + 4/D + 4/E

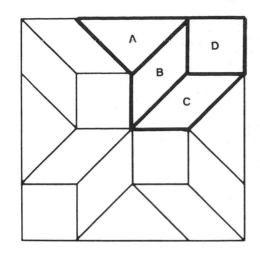

2/B + 2/C

2/B + 2/C

4/D

4/A

98 "Illusion"

ADVANCED

TEMPLATE NUMBERS

	10" block	12" block	14" block
A	41	43	12
B	162	163	164
C	201	202	203
D	69	71	84

BUILDING THE BLOCK

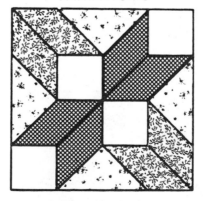

VARIATIONS

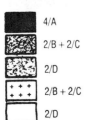

4/A

2/B + 2/C

2/D

2/B + 2/C

2/D

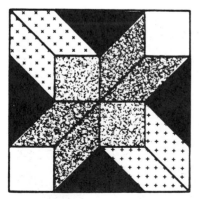

2/B + 2/C

2/B + 2/C

4/A

4/D

2/B + 2/C

2/B + 2/C

4/A + 4/D

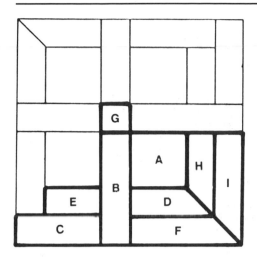

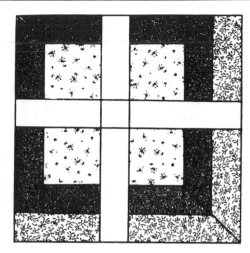

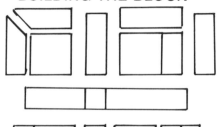

	2/C + 2/D + 2/E + 2/H
	2/C
	4/A
	2/B + 2/C

99 "Cross-Off"

ADVANCED

BUILDING THE BLOCK

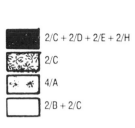

TEMPLATE NUMBERS

	10" block	12" block	14" block
A	41	43	12
B	115	117	119
C	108	104	109
D	95	96	97
E	87	88	89
F	204	205	206
G	36	37	32
H	171	172	173
I	20	21	22

VARIATIONS

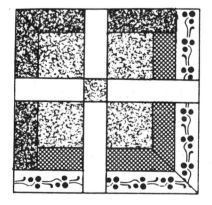

	1/D + 2/E + 1/H
	2/C + 1/D + 1/H
	4/A
	2/C
	2/B + 2/C

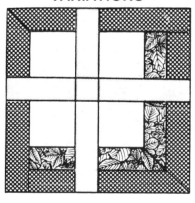

	4/C + 1/D + 1/H
	1/D + 2/E + 1/H
	2/B + 2/C
	4/A

	2/C + 2/D + 2/E + 2/H
	2/B
	3/A
	1/A + 4/C

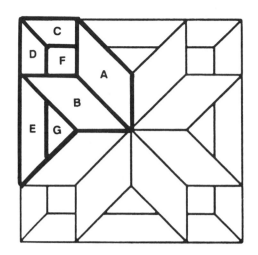

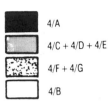

4/A

4/C + 4/D + 4/E

4/F + 4/G

4/B

100
"North Star"

ADVANCED

TEMPLATE NUMBERS

	10" block	12" block	14" block
A	201	202	203
B	162	163	164
C	28	29	30
D	195	196	197
E	180	182	184
F	36	37	32
G	153	74	75

BUILDING THE BLOCK

VARIATIONS

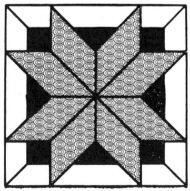

4/C + 4/D + 4/E

4/A + 4/B

4/F + 4/G

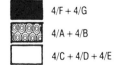

4/F + 4/G

4/A + 4/B

4/C + 4/D + 4/E

4/F + 4/G

2/A + 2/B + 2/C + 2/D + 2/E

2/A + 2/B + 2/C + 2/D + 2/E

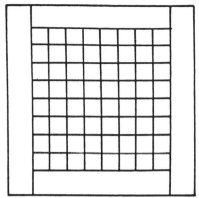

View A. Straight-set blocks

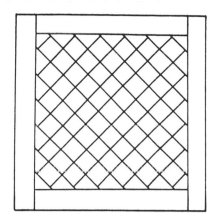

View B. On point

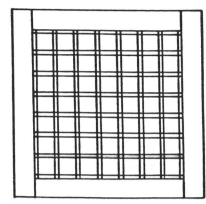

View C. Straight set with lattice

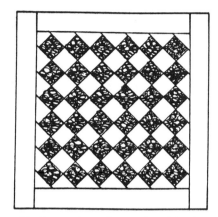

View D. On point, alternating blocks

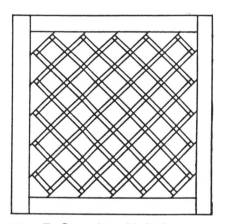

View E. On point with lattice

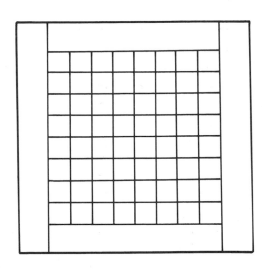

View A.
Blocks, Straight Set

QUILT LAYOUTS
(all measurements in inches)

	Block Size	Blocks Across	Blocks Down	Width of Borders	Size of Finished Quilt
Crib	10	4	5	5	50 × 60
	12	3	4	6	48 × 60
	14	3	4	3	48 × 62
Twin	10	5	8	11	72 × 102
	12	4	7	11	70 × 106
	14	4	6	8	72 × 100
Double	10	6	8	12	84 × 104
	12	5	7	12	84 × 108
	14	5	6	8	86 × 100
Queen	10	6	8	14	88 × 108
	12	5	7	13	86 × 110
	14	5	6	10	90 × 104
King	10	8	8	14	108 × 108
	12	7	7	12	108 × 108
	14	6	6	12	108 × 108
Square Tablecloth	10	5	5	7	64 × 64
	12	4	4	8	64 × 64
	14	4	4	4	64 × 64
Oblong Tablecloth	10	4	6	7	54 × 74
	12	4	5	6	60 × 72
	14	3	4	8	58 × 72

See Appendix C, Yardage Chart for Templates and Backing
See Appendix D, Borders

	Block Size	Total Blocks	Borders Cut Widths (in.)				Yardages (yds.)			
			1st Border (Inner)	2nd Border	3rd Border	4th Border	1st Border (Inner)	2nd Border	3rd Border	4th Border
Crib	10	20	2	5½	—	—	½	1¼	—	—
	12	12	2½	6	—	—	¾	1½	—	—
	14	12	5	—	—	—	1¼	—	—	—
Twin	10	40	2	3½	2	7	¾	1	¾	2
	12	28	2	3½	2	7	¾	1	¾	2
	14	24	2	3	6	—	¾	1	1¾	—
Double	10	48	2	3½	2	8	¾	1¼	¾	2½
	12	35	2	3½	2	8	¾	1¼	¾	2½
	14	30	2	3	6	—	¾	1	2	—
Queen	10	48	2½	4½	2½	8	1	1½	1	2½
	12	35	2	4½	2	8	¾	1½	¾	2½
	14	30	2	3½	7½	—	¾	1¼	2¼	—
King	10	64	2½	4½	2½	8	1	1¾	1	3
	12	49	2	3½	2	8	¾	1½	¾	3
	14	36	2	3½	2	8	¾	1½	¾	3
Square Tablecloth	10	25	2½	7	—	—	¾	1¾	—	—
	12	16	2	3	6	—	¾	1	1½	—
	14	16	1½	5	—	—	½	1¼	—	—
Oblong Tablecloth	10	24	2½	7	—	—	¾	1½	—	—
	12	20	2½	6	—	—	¾	1½	—	—
	14	12	2	3	6	—	½	¾	1½	—

Cutting Notes

Cutting Borders

☐ To cut length of outer borders, add 6" to finished sizes of quilt.
☐ Cut all other borders to finished quilt size.
☐ Trim as needed.
☐ All outer borders include 1 3/4" extra to turn back for finished edge.

Yardage Notes

☐ All yardages include a small amount for shrinkage and waste.
☐ Yardages are for pieced borders, to conserve fabric. You may prefer an unpieced border, especially on wider borders. Use the longest side of your finished quilt to determine how many yards to buy.

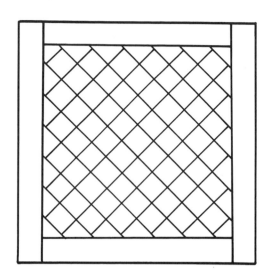

View B.
On Point

QUILT LAYOUTS

(all measurements in inches)

	Block Size	Blocks Across	Blocks Down	Width of Borders	Size of Finished Quilt
Crib	10	3	4	3	49 × 64
	12	2	3	6	47 × 64
	14	2	3	4	49 × 69
Twin	10	4	6	9	76 × 104
	12	3	5	9	70 × 104
	14	3	5	4	69 × 108
Double	10	5	6	9	90 × 104
	12	4	5	9	87 × 104
	14	3	4	12	85 × 104
Queen	10	5	6	10	92 × 106
	12	4	5	11	91 × 108
	14	3	4	14	89 × 108
King	10	6	6	12	110 × 110
	12	5	5	12	110 × 110
	14	4	4	15	110 × 110
Square Tablecloth	10	4	4	4	66 × 66
	12	3	3	7	66 × 66
	14	3	3	3	67 × 67
Oblong Tablecloth	10	3	4	8	59 × 73
	12	3	4	3	58 × 75
	14	2	3	8	57 × 77

**See Appendix C, Yardage Chart for Templates and Backing
See Appendix D, Borders**

	Block Size	Total Blocks	Total Triangles		Borders Cut Widths (in.)				Yardages (yds.)				
			Edges	Corners	1st Border (Inner)	2nd Border	3rd Border	4th Border	Triangles	1st Border (Inner)	2nd Border	3rd Border	4th Border
Crib	10	18	10	4	5	—	—	—	¾	1¼	—	—	—
	12	8	6	4	2½	6	—	—	1	¾	1½	—	—
	14	8	6	4	1½	5	—	—	1½	½	1¼	—	—
Twin	10	39	16	4	2	3½	6½	—	1¼	¾	1	1¾	—
	12	23	12	4	2	3½	6½	—	1½	¾	1	1¾	—
	14	23	12	4	1½	5	—	—	2	½	1½	—	—
Double	10	50	18	4	2	3½	6½	—	1¼	¾	1¼	2	—
	12	32	14	4	2	3½	6½	—	1¾	¾	1¼	2	—
	14	18	10	4	2	3½	2	8	2	¾	1¼	¾	2½
Queen	10	50	18	4	2	3½	7½	—	1½	¾	1¼	2¼	—
	12	32	14	4	2	3½	2	7	1¾	¾	1¼	¾	2¼
	14	18	10	4	2½	4½	2½	8	2	1	1½	1	2½
King	10	61	20	4	2	3½	2	8	1¾	¾	1½	¾	3
	12	41	16	4	2	3½	2	8	1¾	¾	1½	¾	3
	14	25	12	4	2½	4½	2½	9	2	1	1¾	1	3½
Square Tablecloth	10	25	12	4	1½	5	—	—	1	½	1¼	—	—
	12	13	8	4	2½	7	—	—	1	¾	1¾	—	—
	14	13	8	4	5	—	—	—	1½	1¼	—	—	—
Oblong Tablecloth	10	18	10	4	2	3	6	—	¾	½	¾	1½	—
	12	18	10	4	5	—	—	—	1½	1¼	—	—	—
	14	8	6	4	2	3	6	—	1½	½	¾	1½	—

Cutting Notes

Block Sizes	Triangles	
	Edges	Corners
10	12 x 12	9 x 9
12	14 x 14	10½ x 10½
14	16 x 16	11¾ x 11¾

Cut squares to form two triangles ⟶

Cutting Borders

☐ To cut length of outer borders, add 6" to finished sizes of quilt.
☐ Cut all other borders to finished quilt size.
☐ Trim as needed.
☐ All outer borders include 1 3/4" extra to turn back for finished edge.

Yardage Notes

☐ All yardages include a small amount for shrinkage and waste.
☐ Yardages are for pieced borders, to conserve fabric. You may prefer an unpieced border, especially on wider borders. Use the longest side of your finished quilt to determine how many yards to buy.

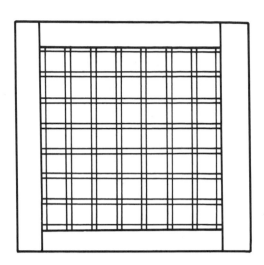

View C.
Blocks and Lattice

QUILT LAYOUTS
(all measurements in inches)

	Block Size	Blocks Across	Blocks Down	Width of Borders	Size of Finished Quilt
Crib	10	3	4	5	48 × 60
	12	3	4	2	50 × 64
	14	2	3	5	47 × 64
Twin	10	4	7	10	70 × 106
	12	4	6	7	74 × 103
	14	3	5	8	70 × 104
Double	10	5	7	10	82 × 106
	12	4	5	14	88 × 103
	14	4	5	8	87 × 104
Queen	10	5	7	12	86 × 110
	12	5	6	8	91 × 105
	14	4	5	9	89 × 106
King	10	7	7	11	108 × 108
	12	6	6	9	107 × 107
	14	5	5	10	108 × 108
Square Tablecloth	10	4	4	7	64 × 64
	12	3	3	9	64 × 64
	14	3	3	5	64 × 64
Oblong Tablecloth	10	4	5	5	60 × 72
	12	3	4	6	58 × 72
	14	2	3	9	55 × 72

See Appendix C, Yardage Chart for Templates and Backing
See Appendix D, Borders

	Block Size	Total Blocks	Lattice		Borders Cut Widths (in.)				Yardages (yds.)					
			Total Strips	Total Squares	1st Border (Inner)	2nd Border	3rd Border	4th Border	Lattice Strips	Lattice Squares	1st Border (Inner)	2nd Border	3rd Border	4th Border
Crib	10	12	31	20	2	5½	—	—	¾	¼	½	1¼	—	—
	12	12	31	20	4	—	—	—	1¼	¼	1	—	—	—
	14	6	17	12	2	5½	—	—	1	¼	½	1¼	—	—
Twin	10	28	67	40	2	3½	7½	—	1¾	¼	½	1	2	—
	12	24	58	35	2½	7	—	—	2	½	¾	2	—	—
	14	15	38	24	2	3	6	—	2	½	¾	1	1¾	—
Double	10	35	82	48	2	3½	7½	—	2	¼	¾	1¼	2¼	—
	12	20	49	30	2½	4½	2½	8	1¾	½	1	1½	1	2½
	14	20	49	30	2	3	6	—	2¼	½	¾	1	2	—
Queen	10	35	82	48	2	3½	2	8	2	¼	¾	1¼	¾	2½
	12	30	71	42	2	3	6	—	2½	½	¾	1	2	—
	14	20	49	30	2	3½	6½	—	2¼	½	¾	1¼	2	—
King	10	49	112	64	2	3½	2	7	2¼	½	¾	1½	¾	2½
	12	36	84	49	2	3½	6½	—	2¾	½	¾	1½	2½	—
	14	25	60	36	2	3½	7½	—	2¾	½	¾	1½	2¾	—
Square Tablecloth	10	16	40	25	2½	7	—	—	1	¼	¾	1¾	—	—
	12	9	24	16	2	3½	6½	—	1	¼	¾	1	1¾	—
	14	9	24	16	2	5½	—	—	1½	¼	¾	1½	—	—
Oblong Tablecloth	10	20	49	30	2	5½	—	—	1½	¼	½	1¼	—	—
	12	12	31	20	2½	6	—	—	1¼	¼	¾	1½	—	—
	14	6	17	12	2	3½	6½	—	1	¼	½	1	1½	—

Cutting Notes

Block Size	Lattice	
	Strips	Squares
10	2½ x 10½	2½ x 2½
12	3 x 12½	3 x 3
14	3½ x 14½	3½ x 3½

Cutting Borders

☐ To cut length of outer borders, add 6" to finished sizes of quilt.
☐ Cut all other borders to finished quilt size.
☐ Trim as needed.
☐ All outer borders include 1 3/4" extra to turn back for finished edge.

Yardage Notes

☐ All yardages include a small amount for shrinkage and waste.
☐ Yardages are for pieced borders, to conserve fabric. You may prefer an unpieced border, especially on wider borders. Use the longest side of your finished quilt to determine how many yards to buy.

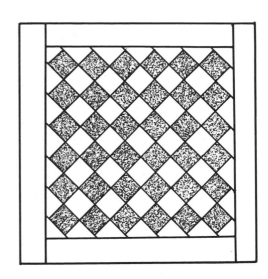

View D.
On Point with
Alternating Blocks

QUILT LAYOUTS
(all measurements in inches)

	Block Size	Blocks Across	Blocks Down	Width of Borders	Size of Finished Quilt
Crib	10	3	4	3	49 × 64
	12	2	3	6	47 × 64
	14	2	3	4	49 × 69
Twin	10	4	6	9	76 × 104
	12	3	5	9	70 × 104
	14	3	5	4	69 × 108
Double	10	5	6	9	90 × 104
	12	4	5	9	87 × 104
	14	3	4	12	85 × 104
Queen	10	5	6	10	92 × 106
	12	4	5	11	91 × 108
	14	3	4	14	89 × 108
King	10	6	6	12	110 × 110
	12	5	5	12	110 × 110
	14	4	4	15	110 × 110
Square Tablecloth	10	4	4	4	66 × 66
	12	3	3	7	66 × 66
	14	3	3	3	67 × 67
Oblong Tablecloth	10	3	4	8	59 × 73
	12	3	4	3	58 × 75
	14	2	3	8	57 × 77

See Appendix C, Yardage Chart for Templates and Backing
See Appendix D, Borders

	Block Size	Total Blocks		Total Triangles		Borders Cut Widths (in.)				Yardages (yds.)				
		Pieced	Unpieced	Edges	Corners	1st Border (Inner)	2nd Border	3rd Border	4th Border	Triangles and Unpieced Blocks	1st Border (Inner)	2nd Border	3rd Border	4th Border
Crib	10	12	6	10	4	5	—	—	—	1½	1¼	—	—	—
	12	6	2	6	4	2½	6	—	—	1½	¾	1½	—	—
	14	6	2	6	4	1½	5	—	—	2	½	1¼	—	—
Twin	10	24	15	16	4	2	3½	6½	—	3	¾	1	1¾	—
	12	15	8	12	4	2	3½	6½	—	2¾	¾	1	1¾	—
	14	15	8	12	4	1½	5	—	—	3¾	½	1½	—	—
Double	10	30	20	18	4	2	3½	6½	—	3½	¾	1¼	2	—
	12	20	12	14	4	2	3½	6½	—	3¼	¾	1¼	2	—
	14	12	6	10	4	2	3½	2	8	3½	¾	1¼	¾	2½
Queen	10	30	20	18	4	2	3½	7½	—	3¾	¾	1¼	2¼	—
	12	20	12	14	4	2	3½	2	7	3¼	¾	1¼	¾	2¼
	14	12	6	10	4	2½	4½	2½	8	3½	1	1½	1	2½
King	10	36	25	20	4	2	3½	2	8	4¾	¾	1½	¾	3
	12	25	16	16	4	2	3½	2	8	4¼	¾	1½	¾	3
	14	16	9	12	4	2½	4½	2½	9	4¼	1	1¾	1	3½
Square Tablecloth	10	16	9	12	4	1½	5	—	—	2	½	1¼	—	—
	12	9	4	8	4	2½	7	—	—	2	¾	1¾	—	—
	14	9	4	8	4	5	—	—	—	2½	1¼	—	—	—
Oblong Tablecloth	10	12	6	10	4	2	3	6	—	1½	½	¾	1½	—
	12	12	6	10	4	5	—	—	—	2½	1¼	—	—	—
	14	6	2	6	4	2	3	6	—	2	½	¾	1½	—

Cutting Notes

Block Size	Triangles		Block Size	Unpieced Blocks
	Edges	Corners		
10	12 x 12	9 x 9	10	10½ x 10½
12	14 x 14	10½ x 10½	12	12½ x 12½
14	16 x 16	11¾ x 11¾	14	14½ x 14½

Cut squares to form two triangles ➤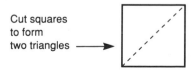

Cutting Borders

☐ To cut length of outer borders, add 6" to finished sizes of quilt.
☐ Cut all other borders to finished quilt size.
☐ Trim as needed.
☐ All outer borders include 1 3/4" extra to turn back for finished edge.

Yardage Notes

☐ All yardages include a small amount for shrinkage and waste.
☐ Yardages are for pieced borders, to conserve fabric. You may prefer an unpieced border, especially on wider borders. Use the longest side of your finished quilt to determine how many yards to buy.

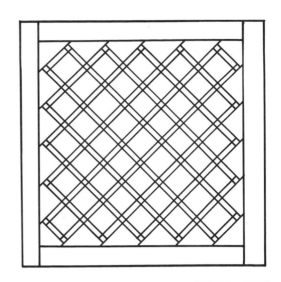

View E.
On Point with Lattice

QUILT LAYOUTS

(all measurements in inches)

	Block Size	Blocks Across	Blocks Down	Width of Borders	Size of Finished Quilt
Crib	10	2	3	4	46 × 63
	12	2	3	2	50 × 70
	14	1	2	8	45 × 69
Twin	10	3	5	8	71 × 105
	12	3	5	2	70 × 111
	14	2	3	12	77 × 101
Double	10	4	5	7	86 × 103
	12	3	4	10	87 × 106
	14	3	4	4	85 × 109
Queen	10	4	5	8	88 × 105
	12	3	4	11	88 × 108
	14	3	4	5	87 × 111
King	10	5	5	10	109 × 109
	12	4	4	11	108 × 108
	14	4	4	4	109 × 109
Square Tablecloth	10	3	3	5	65 × 65
	12	2	2	10	66 × 66
	14	2	2	6	65 × 65
Oblong Tablecloth	10	3	4	2	59 × 76
	12	2	3	5	56 × 76
	14	2	3	2	57 × 81

See Appendix C, Yardage Chart for Templates and Backing
See Appendix D, Borders

	Block Size	Total Blocks	Total Triangles		Lattice		Borders Cut Widths (in.)				Yardages (in.)						
			Edges	Corners	Total Strips	Total Squares	1st Border (Inner)	2nd	3rd	4th	Triangles	Lattice Strips	Lattice Squares	1st Border (Inner)	2nd	3rd	4th
Crib	10	8	6	4	24	17	1½	5	—	—	1½	¾	¼	½	1¼	—	—
	12	8	6	4	24	17	4	—	—	—	2¼	1	¼	1	—	—	—
	14	2	2	4	8	7	2	3	6	—	1¼	½	¼	½	¾	1½	—
Twin	10	23	12	4	60	38	2	3	6	—	2¼	1½	¼	¾	1	1¾	—
	12	23	12	4	60	38	4	—	—	—	4¼	2½	½	1¼	—	—	—
	14	8	6	4	24	17	2	3½	2	8	3	¾	¼	¾	1	¾	2¼
Double	10	32	14	4	80	49	2½	7	—	—	2¾	2	½	1	2¼	—	—
	12	18	10	4	48	31	2	3½	7½	—	3½	1¾	½	¾	1¼	2¼	—
	14	18	10	4	48	31	1½	5	—	—	4½	2¼	½	½	1¾	—	—
Queen	10	32	14	4	80	49	2	3	6	—	2¾	2	½	¾	1	2	—
	12	18	10	4	48	31	2	3½	2	7	3½	1¾	½	¾	1¼	¾	2¼
	14	18	10	4	48	31	2	5½	—	—	4½	2¼	½	¾	1¾	—	—
King	10	41	16	4	100	60	2	3½	7½	—	2¾	2¼	½	¾	1½	2¾	—
	12	25	12	4	64	40	2	3½	2	7	4¼	2½	½	¾	1½	¾	2½
	14	25	12	4	64	40	1½	5	—	—	5¼	2¾	½	¾	2	—	—
Square Tablecloth	10	13	8	4	36	24	2	5½	—	—	1½	1	¼	¾	1½	—	—
	12	5	4	4	16	12	2	3½	7½	—	1½	1	¼	¾	1	2	—
	14	5	4	4	16	12	2½	6	—	—	2¼	1	¼	¾	1½	—	—
Oblong Tablecloth	10	18	10	4	48	31	4	—	—	—	2¼	1	¼	1	—	—	—
	12	8	6	4	24	17	2	5½	—	—	2¼	1	¼	½	1¼	—	—
	14	8	6	4	24	17	4	—	—	—	3	1½	¼	1	—	—	—

Cutting Notes

Block Sizes	Triangles		Block Size	Lattice	
	Edges	Corners		Strips	Squares
10	18¾ x 18¾	11⅞ x 11⅞	10	2½ x 10½	2½ x 2½
12	22⅜ x 22⅜	14⅛ x 14⅛	12	3 x 12½	3 x 3
14	25¾ x 25¾	16¼ x 16¼	14	3½ x 14½	3½ x 3½

Cut squares to form two triangles ⟶

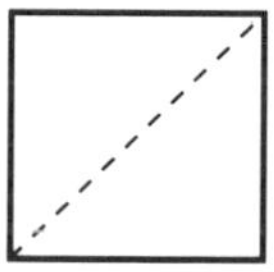

Cutting Borders

☐ To cut length of outer borders, add 6" to finished sizes of quilt.
☐ Cut all other borders to finished quilt size.
☐ Trim as needed.
☐ All outer borders include 1 3/4" extra to turn back for finished edge.

Yardage Notes

☐ All yardages include a small amount for shrinkage and waste.
☐ Yardages are for pieced borders, to conserve fabric. You may prefer an unpieced border, especially on wider borders. Use the longest side of your finished quilt to determine how many yards to buy.

YARDAGE CHART FOR TEMPLATES

Template Number	Number of Pieces from: ¼ yard	½ yard	1 yard	Template Number	Number of Pieces from: ¼ yard	½ yard	1 yard	Template Number	Number of Pieces from: ¼ yard	½ yard	1 yard
1	32	72	144	34	10	40	80	67	20	80	160
2	18	48	96	35	140	280	588	68	18	54	126
3	18	42	84	36	96	216	432	69	18	54	126
4	96	216	432	37	63	168	336	70	16	48	96
5	63	168	336	38	54	126	252	71	16	48	96
6	57	133	266	39	48	96	192	72	14	28	70
7	48	96	192	40	28	70	154	73	96	192	384
8	32	80	176	41	28	70	140	74	56	140	280
9	28	70	140	42	24	48	108	75	48	96	216
10	24	48	108	43	24	48	108	76	44	88	176
11	11	44	88	44	10	40	80	77	18	54	126
12	10	40	80	45	10	30	70	78	18	54	126
13	9	27	63	46	8	24	48	79	18	54	108
14	8	24	48	47	8	24	48	80	16	48	96
15	8	16	40	48	18	48	96	81	16	48	96
16	7	14	35	49	15	35	70	82	14	28	70
17	6	12	30	50	12	24	48	83	14	28	70
18	32	72	144	51	80	160	336	84	14	28	70
19	21	49	98	52	56	126	252	85	12	24	60
20	32	72	144	53	36	96	192	86	12	24	48
21	21	56	112	54	16	40	88	87	56	126	252
22	18	42	84	55	14	35	70	88	36	96	192
23	30	70	140	56	12	24	54	89	30	70	140
24	27	54	108	57	12	24	54	90	27	54	108
25	16	40	88	58	5	20	40	91	16	40	88
26	12	24	54	59	32	72	144	92	14	28	63
27	5	20	40	60	21	56	112	93	6	18	42
28	68	153	306	61	18	42	84	94	5	15	30
29	45	120	240	62	102	204	442	95	44	99	198
30	36	72	156	63	96	192	384	96	27	72	144
31	63	168	336	64	56	140	308	97	24	56	112
32	54	126	252	65	48	96	216	98	50	110	220
33	28	70	140	66	44	88	176	99	36	81	171

Template Number	Number of Pieces from:		
	¼ yard	½ yard	1 yard
100	32	72	144
101	21	56	112
102	18	42	84
103	12	24	48
104	24	64	128
105	21	42	84
106	12	30	60
107	10	20	45
108	36	81	153
109	21	49	98
110	18	36	72
111	10	25	55
112	10	25	55
113	8	16	36
114	45	90	189
115	28	63	126
116	24	54	102
117	18	48	96
118	15	35	75
119	15	35	70
120	12	24	48
121	8	20	44
122	32	72	144
123	18	48	96
124	18	42	84
125	18	42	84
126	15	30	60
127	8	20	44
128	24	48	96
129	14	35	77
130	12	24	54
131	28	70	154
132	18	45	90

Template Number	Number of Pieces from:		
	¼ yard	½ yard	1 yard
133	16	32	72
134	7	28	56
135	65	130	273
136	44	99	198
137	27	72	144
138	10	40	80
139	8	24	56
140	7	21	42
141	90	180	378
142	64	144	288
143	45	120	240
144	24	56	112
145	21	42	84
146	12	30	66
147	60	120	252
148	44	99	198
149	40	90	170
150	24	56	112
151	21	42	84
152	12	30	66
153	60	150	330
154	56	140	308
155	48	96	216
156	48	96	216
157	18	54	126
158	16	48	96
159	45	90	189
160	32	72	144
161	21	56	112
162	15	35	70
163	15	30	60
164	8	20	40
165	39	91	195

Template Number	Number of Pieces from:		
	¼ yard	½ yard	1 yard
166	30	60	120
167	20	50	110
168	18	45	90
169	16	32	72
170	6	24	48
171	40	90	180
172	27	72	144
173	24	56	112
174	50	100	210
175	32	72	152
176	32	72	144
177	21	56	112
178	18	42	84
179	15	30	60
180	32	72	144
181	24	64	128
182	21	49	105
183	18	42	84
184	18	42	84
185	15	30	60
186	18	42	84
187	18	42	84
188	15	30	60
189	15	30	60
190	8	20	44
191	8	20	40
192	40	80	168
193	28	63	126
194	18	48	96
195	48	128	272
196	42	112	224
197	36	72	156
198	32	72	144

Template Number	Number of Pieces from:			Template Number	Number of Pieces from:			Template Number	Number of Pieces from:		
	¼ yard	½ yard	1 yard		¼ yard	½ yard	1 yard		¼ yard	½ yard	1 yard
199	21	56	112	207	90	180	378	215	6	24	48
200	18	42	84	208	64	144	288	216	45	90	189
201	18	36	78	209	42	112	224	217	32	72	144
202	15	30	60	210	36	84	168	218	21	56	112
203	8	20	40	211	30	60	120	219	18	42	84
204	32	72	144	212	20	50	110	220	15	30	60
205	18	48	96	213	18	45	90	221	8	20	44
206	18	42	84	214	16	32	72				

Yardage figures are based on 42" of usable fabric width (after shrinkage and removal of selvages). A small amount has been allowed in the length for shrinkage and waste.

YARDAGE AND PIECING GUIDES FOR BACKING

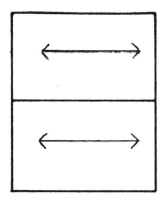

Crib: 3¼ yards.
Oblong tablecloth:
  3¾ yards.

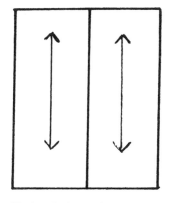

Twin: 6¾ yards.
Square tablecloth:
  4 yards.

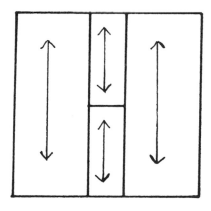

Double: 8½ yards.
Queen: 8½ yards.

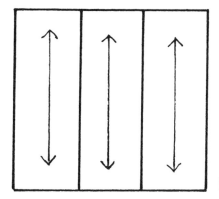

King: 10¼ yards.

Yardage includes small amount for shrinkage and waste.
⟷ indicates lengthwise grain of fabric.

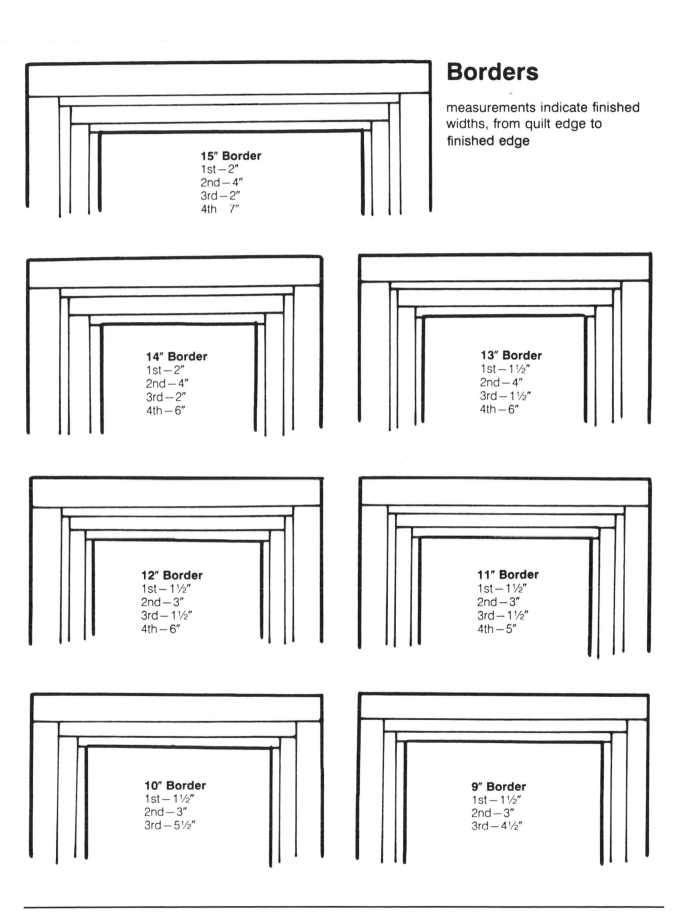

Borders

measurements indicate finished widths, from quilt edge to finished edge

15″ Border
1st — 2″
2nd — 4″
3rd — 2″
4th   7″

14″ Border
1st — 2″
2nd — 4″
3rd — 2″
4th — 6″

13″ Border
1st — 1½″
2nd — 4″
3rd — 1½″
4th — 6″

12″ Border
1st — 1½″
2nd — 3″
3rd — 1½″
4th — 6″

11″ Border
1st — 1½″
2nd — 3″
3rd — 1½″
4th — 5″

10″ Border
1st — 1½″
2nd — 3″
3rd — 5½″

9″ Border
1st — 1½″
2nd — 3″
3rd — 4½″

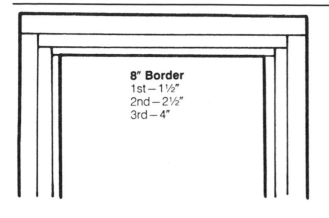

8" Border
1st — 1½"
2nd — 2½"
3rd — 4"

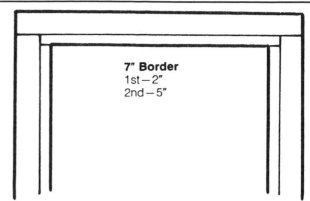

7" Border
1st — 2"
2nd — 5"

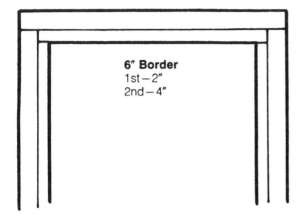

6" Border
1st — 2"
2nd — 4"

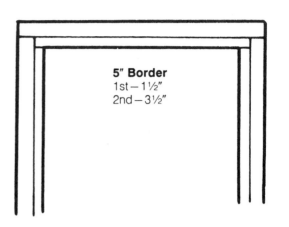

5" Border
1st — 1½"
2nd — 3½"

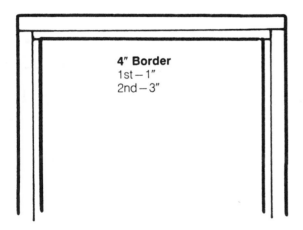

4" Border
1st — 1"
2nd — 3"

3" Border — 3"
or
2" border — 2"

CUT WIDTH OF BORDER STRIPS

Total Border Width	1st Border	2nd Border	3rd Border	4th Border
15"	2½"	4½"	2½"	9*
14"	2½"	4½"	2½"	8*
13"	2"	4½"	2"	8*
12"	2"	3½"	2"	8*
11"	2"	3½"	2"	7*
10"	2"	3½"	7½*	
9"	2"	3½"	6½*	
8"	2"	3"	6*	
7"	2½"	7*		
6"	2½"	6*		
5"	2"	5½*		
4"	1½"	5*		
3"	5*			
2"	4*			

*Includes outer border strip. Cut width includes 1¾" for "binding" turnback.

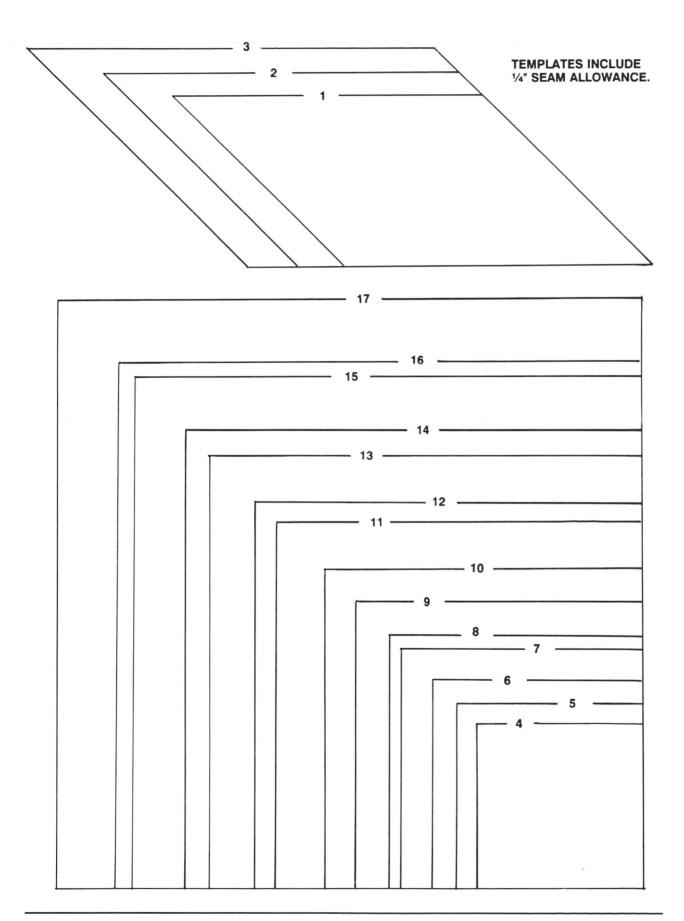

TEMPLATES INCLUDE
¼" SEAM ALLOWANCE.

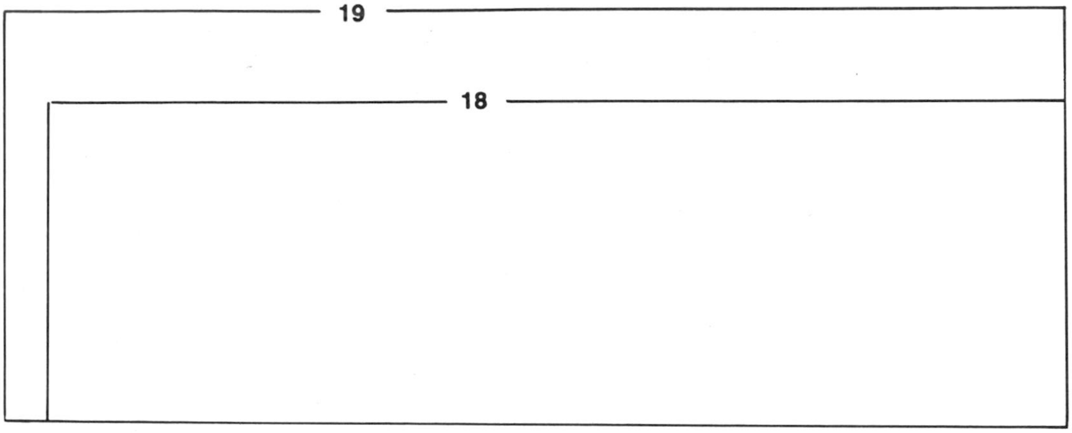

19

18

TEMPLATES INCLUDE ¼" SEAM ALLOWANCE.

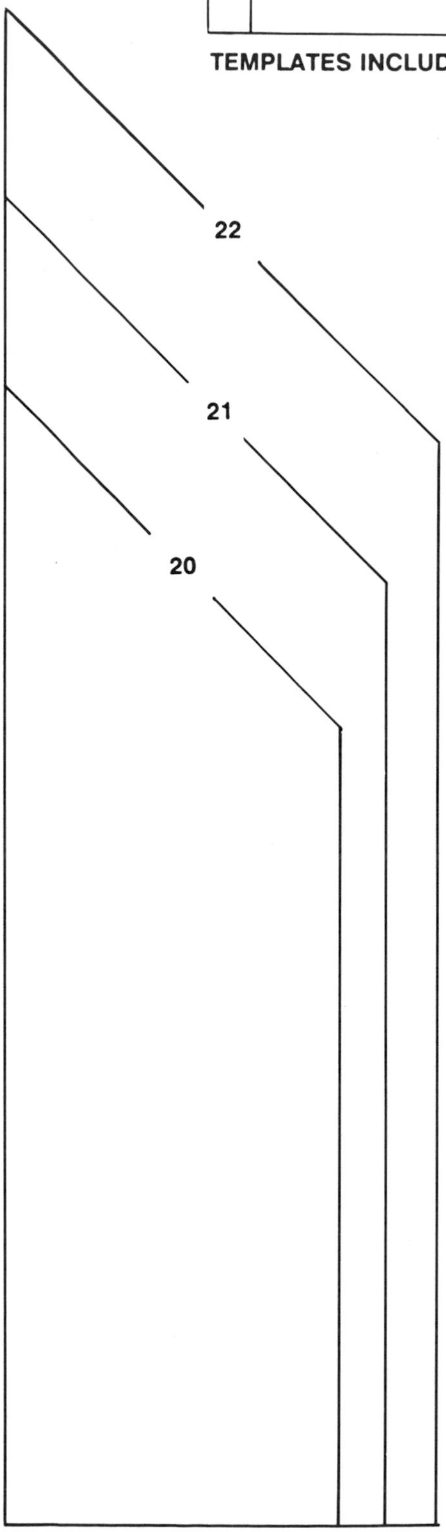

22

21

20

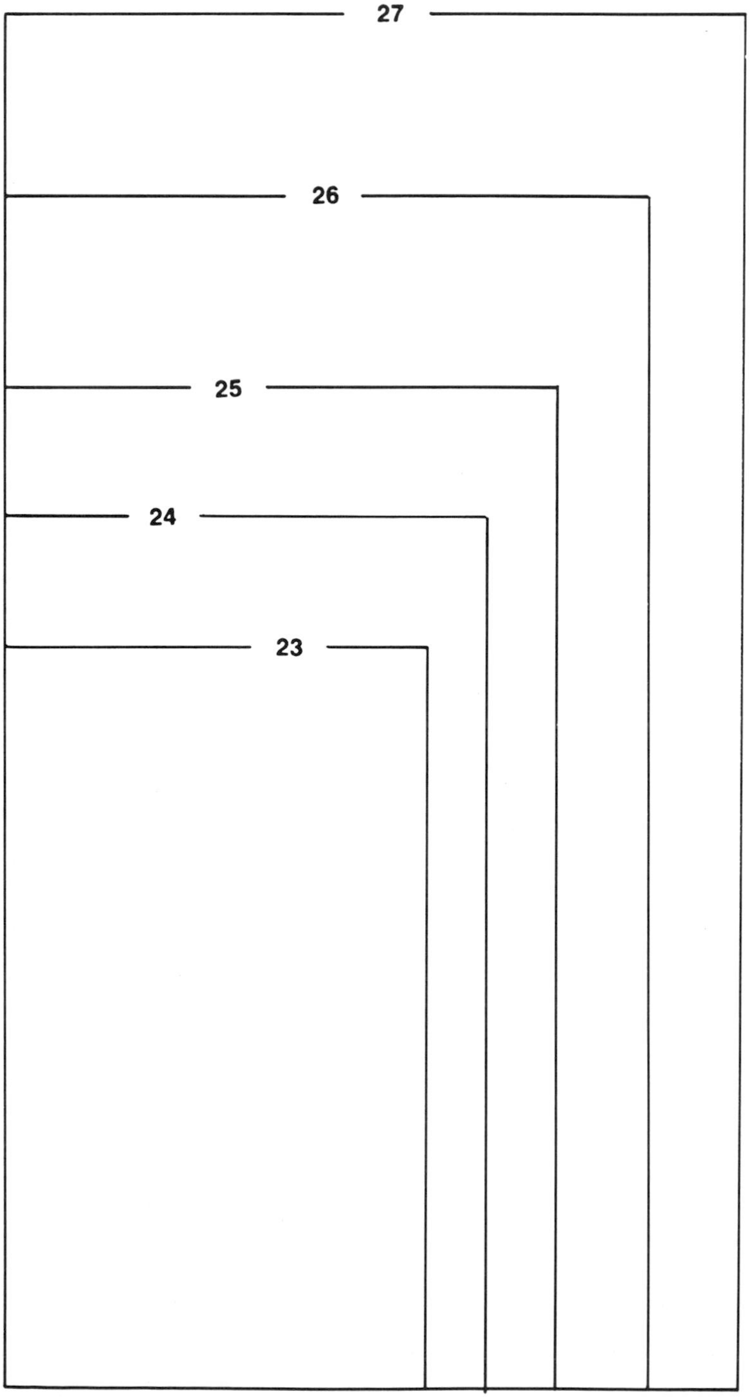

27

26

25

24

23

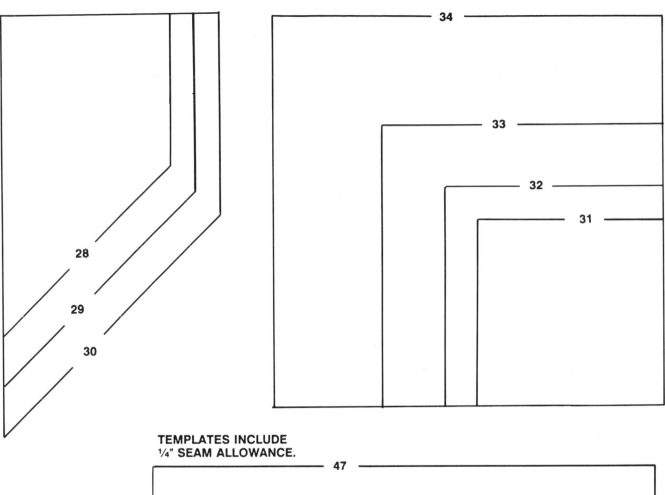

**TEMPLATES INCLUDE
¼" SEAM ALLOWANCE.**

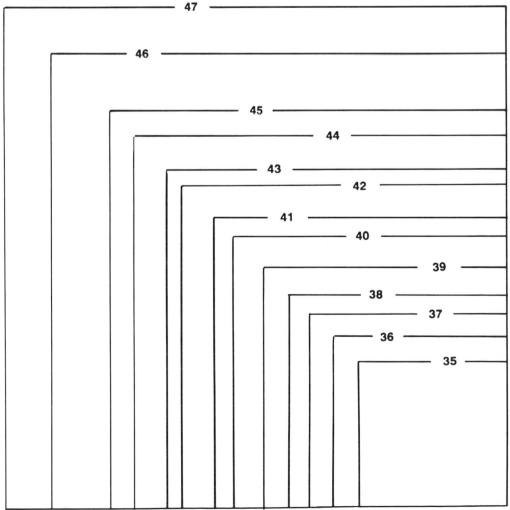

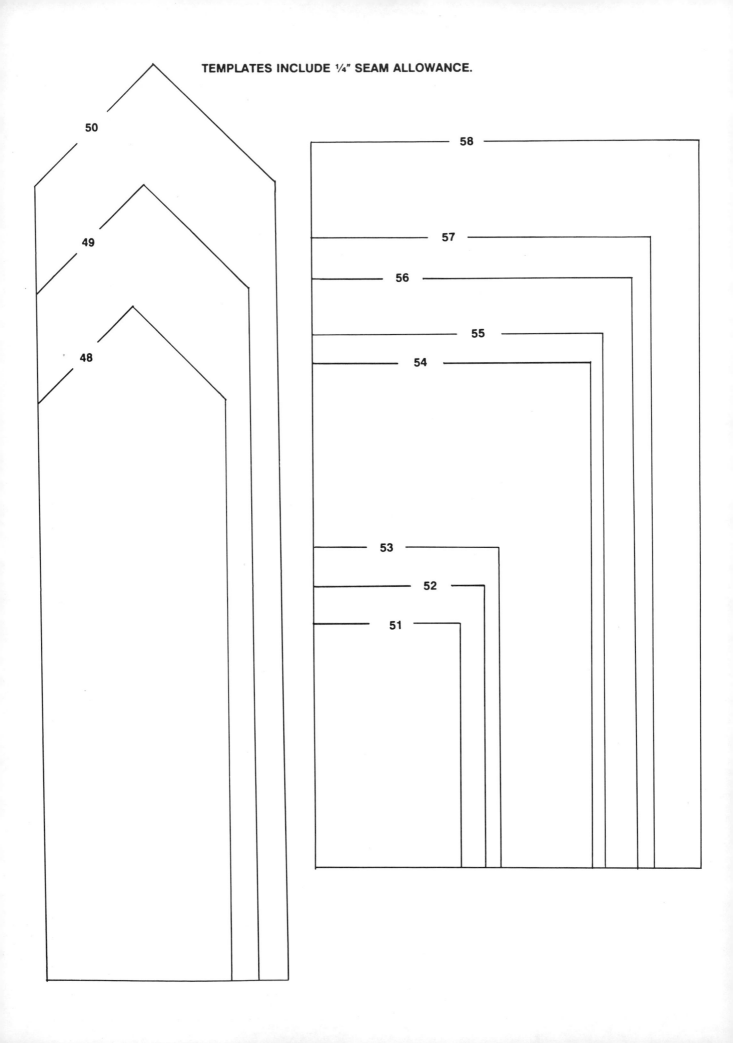

TEMPLATES INCLUDE ¼" SEAM ALLOWANCE.

50

49

48

58

57

56

55

54

53

52

51

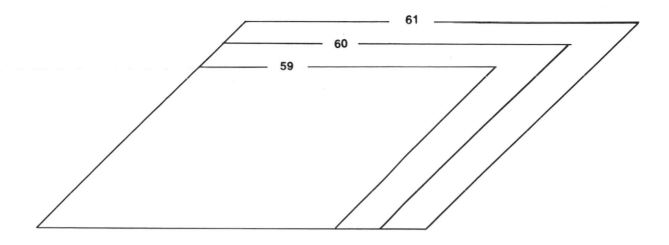

TEMPLATES INCLUDE ¼" SEAM ALLOWANCE.

61

60

59

63

62

65

67

64

69

66

71

86

68

70

84

72

79

83 81

77

85 82

75

78

80

73

76 74

**TEMPLATES INCLUDE
¼″ SEAM ALLOWANCE.**

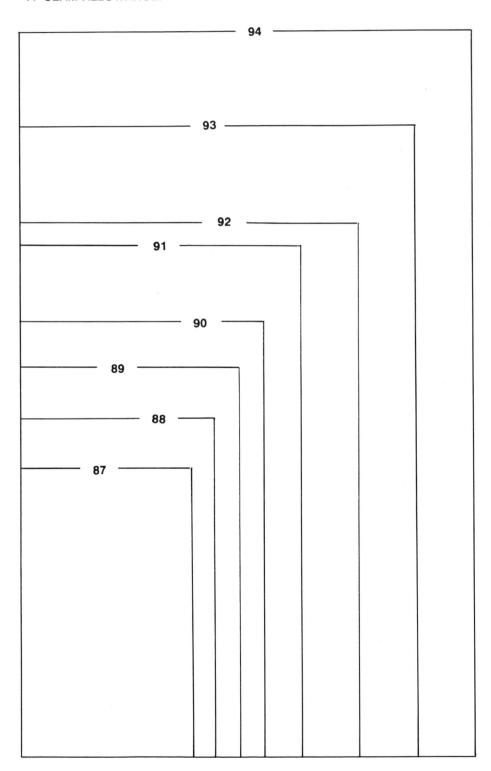

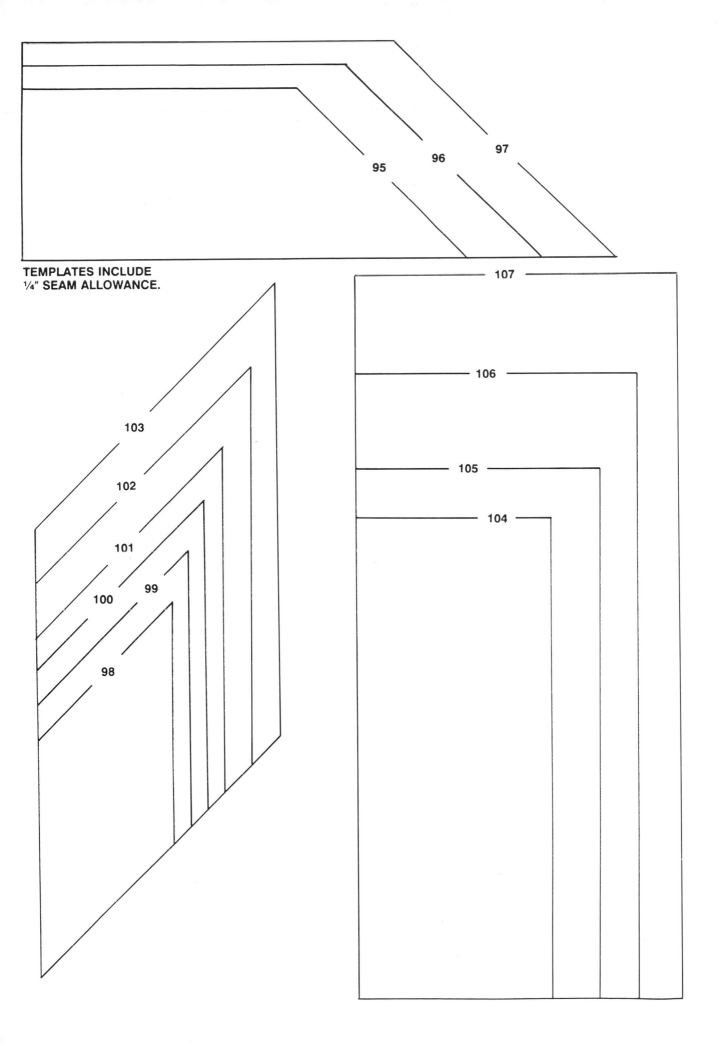

TEMPLATES INCLUDE ¼" SEAM ALLOWANCE.

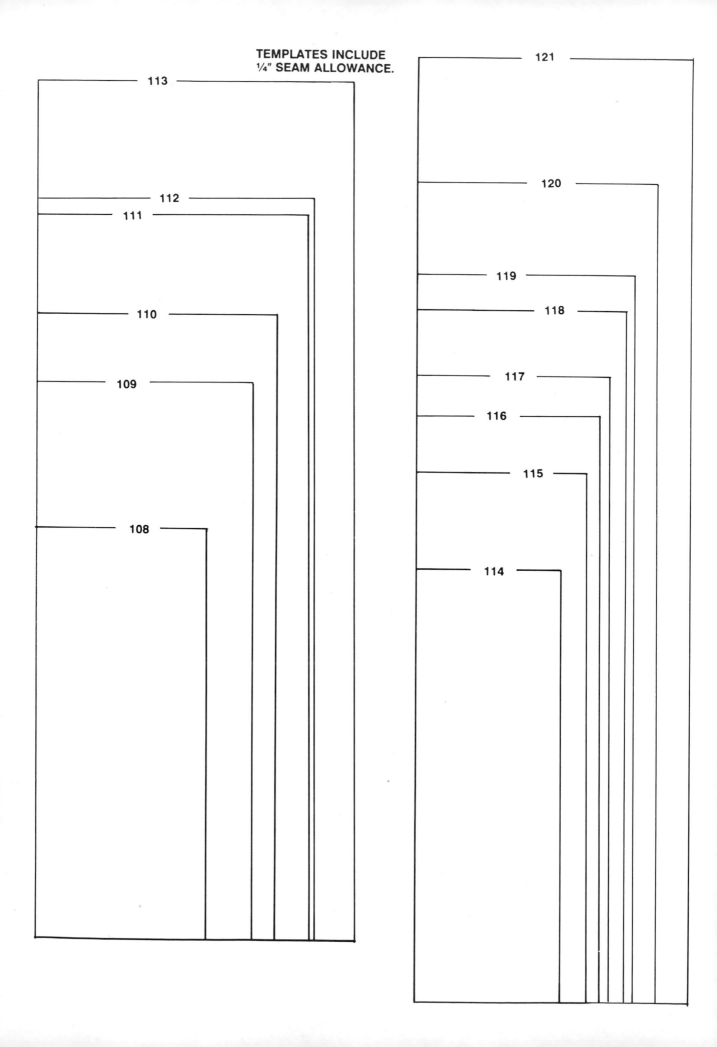

TEMPLATES INCLUDE
¼" SEAM ALLOWANCE.

113

112

111

110

109

108

121

120

119

118

117

116

115

114

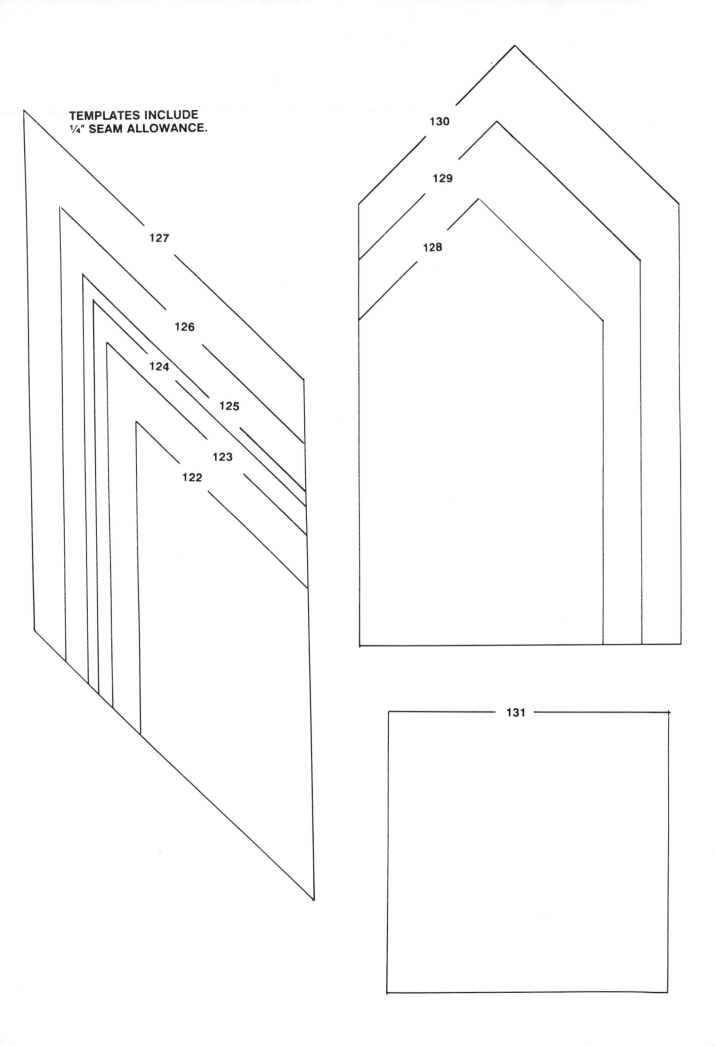

**TEMPLATES INCLUDE
¼" SEAM ALLOWANCE.**

127

126

124

125

123

122

130

129

128

131

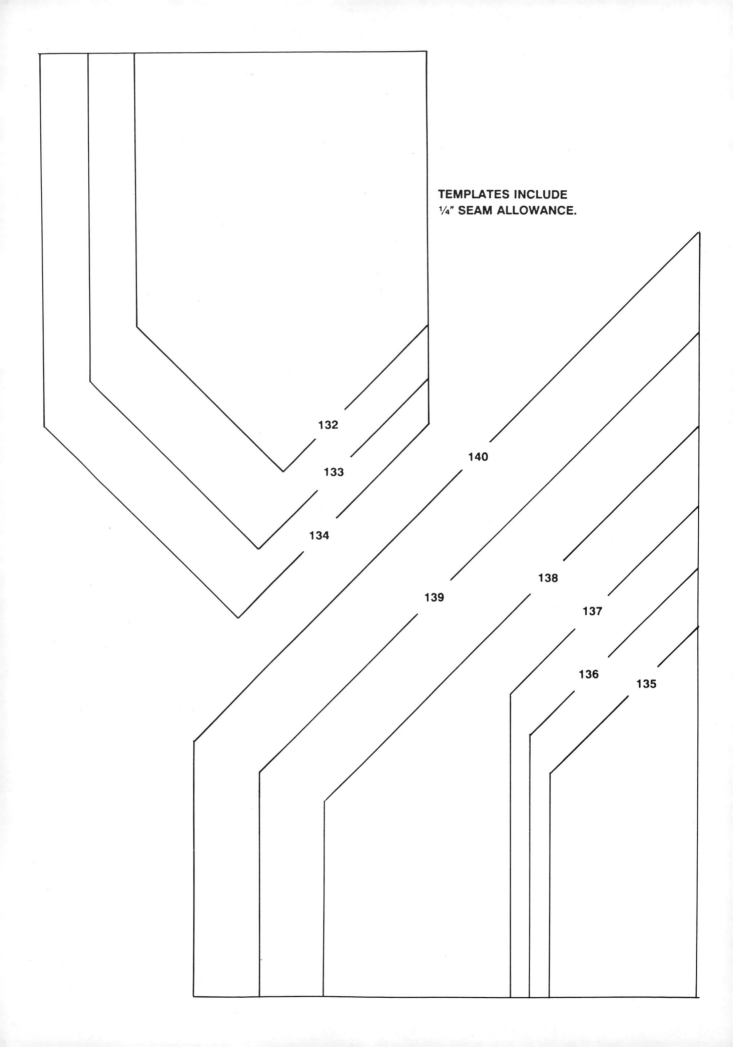

TEMPLATES INCLUDE
¼″ SEAM ALLOWANCE.

132

133

134

140

139

138

137

136

135

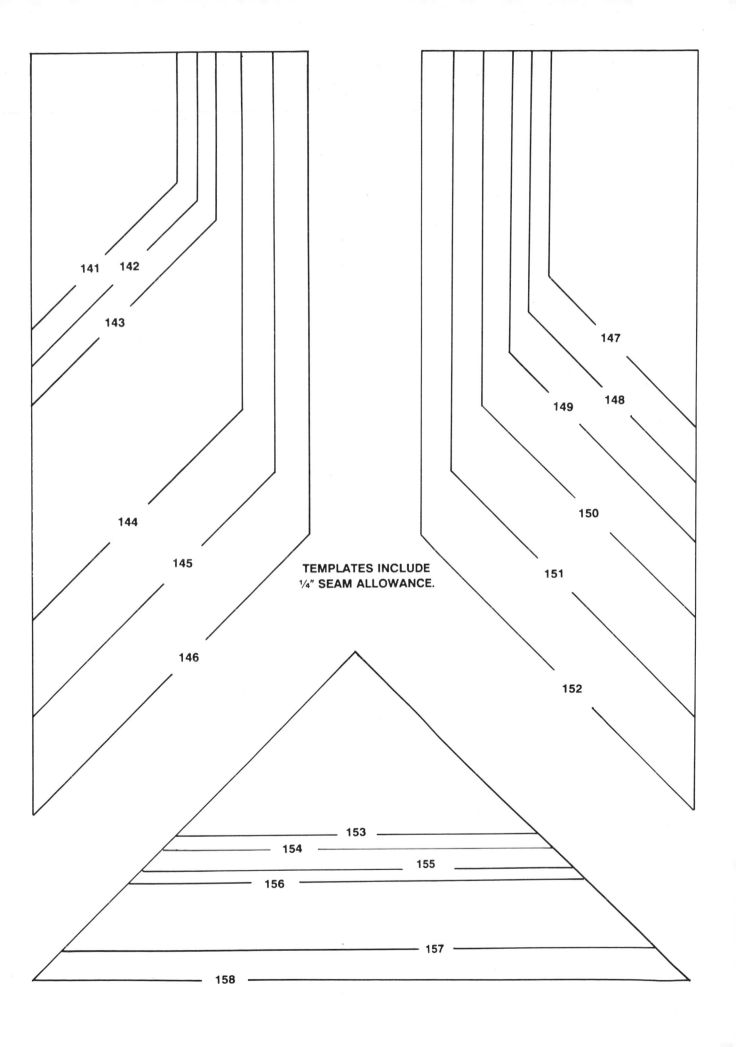

141 142

143

147

148 149

144

150

145

151

146

152

TEMPLATES INCLUDE
¼" SEAM ALLOWANCE.

153

154

155

156

157

158

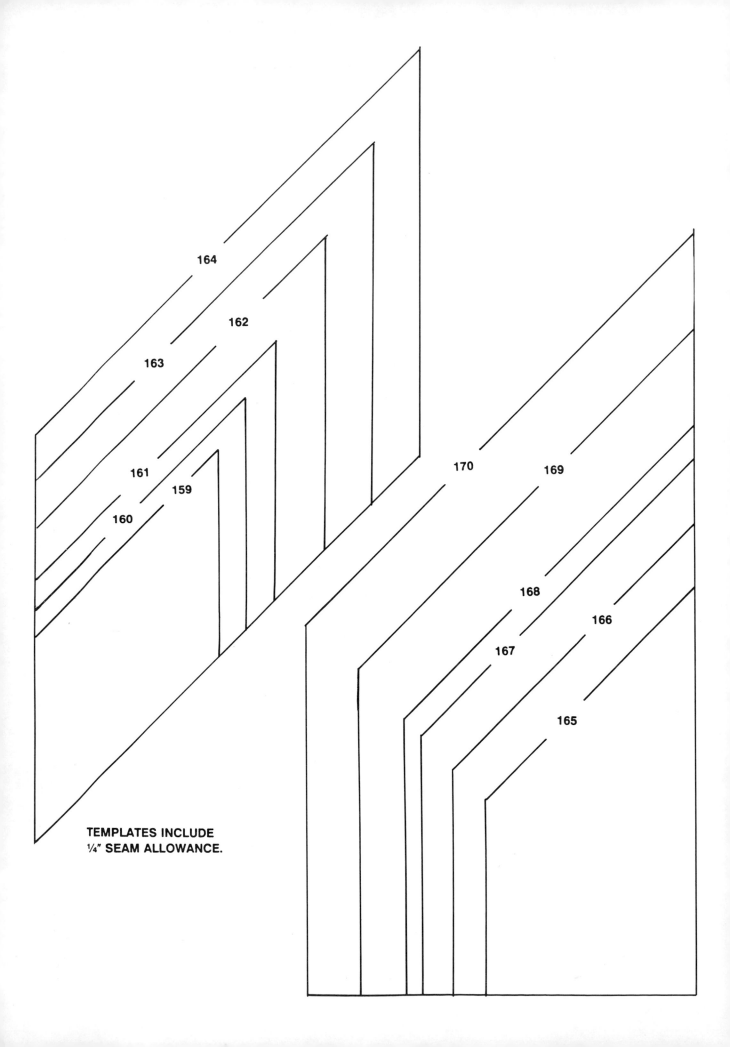

164

162

163

170 169

161 159

168 166

160

167

165

**TEMPLATES INCLUDE
¼" SEAM ALLOWANCE.**

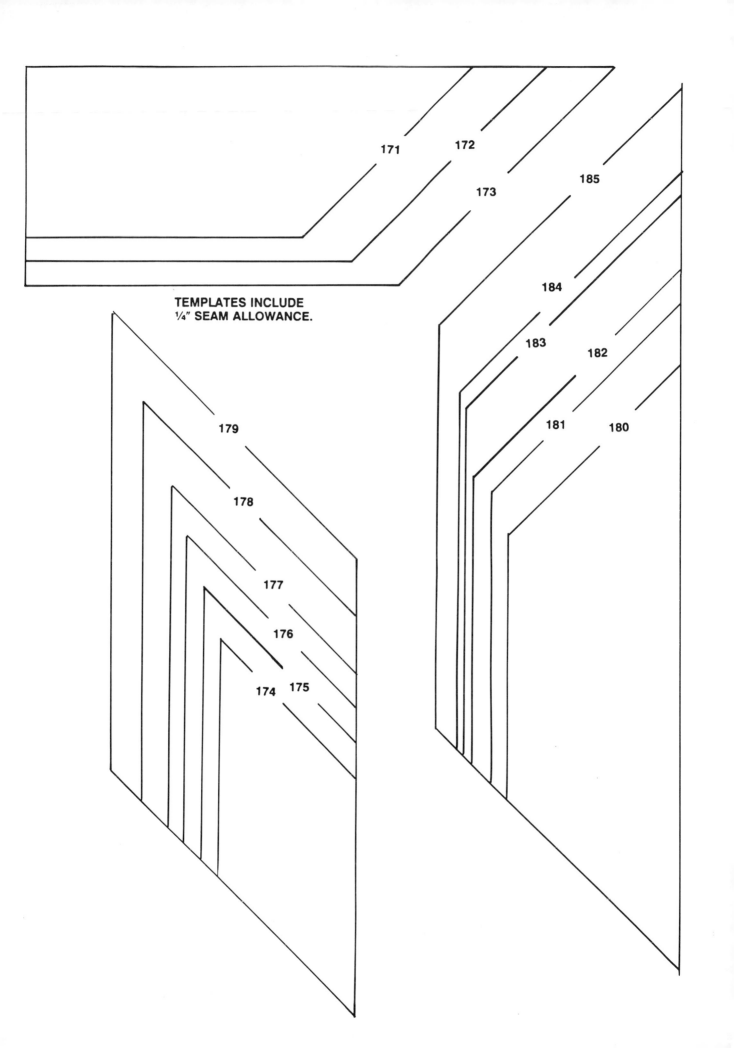

171 172
173 185
184
183 182
179 181 180
178
177
176
174 175

**TEMPLATES INCLUDE
¼" SEAM ALLOWANCE.**

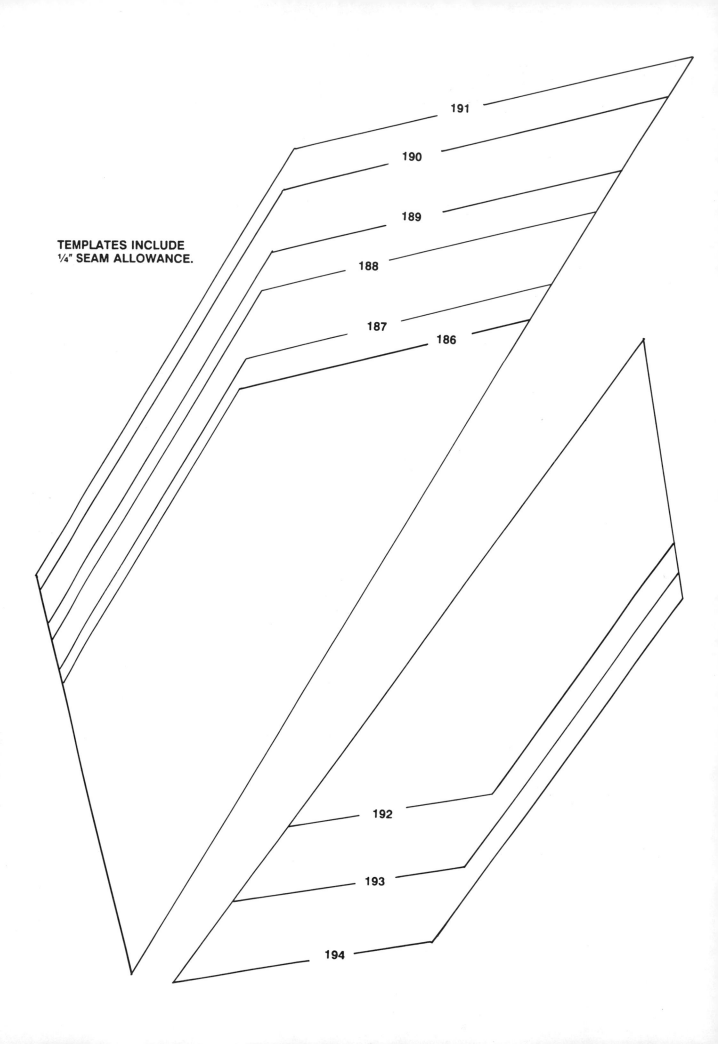

TEMPLATES INCLUDE
¼" SEAM ALLOWANCE.

191

190

189

188

187

186

192

193

194

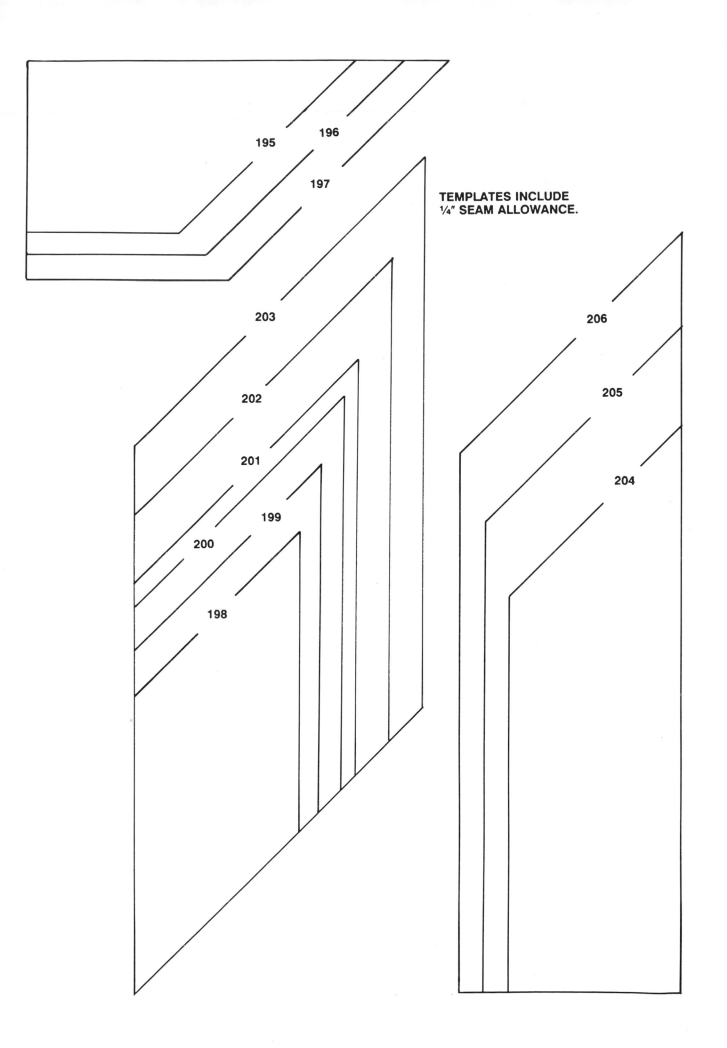

TEMPLATES INCLUDE
¼" SEAM ALLOWANCE.

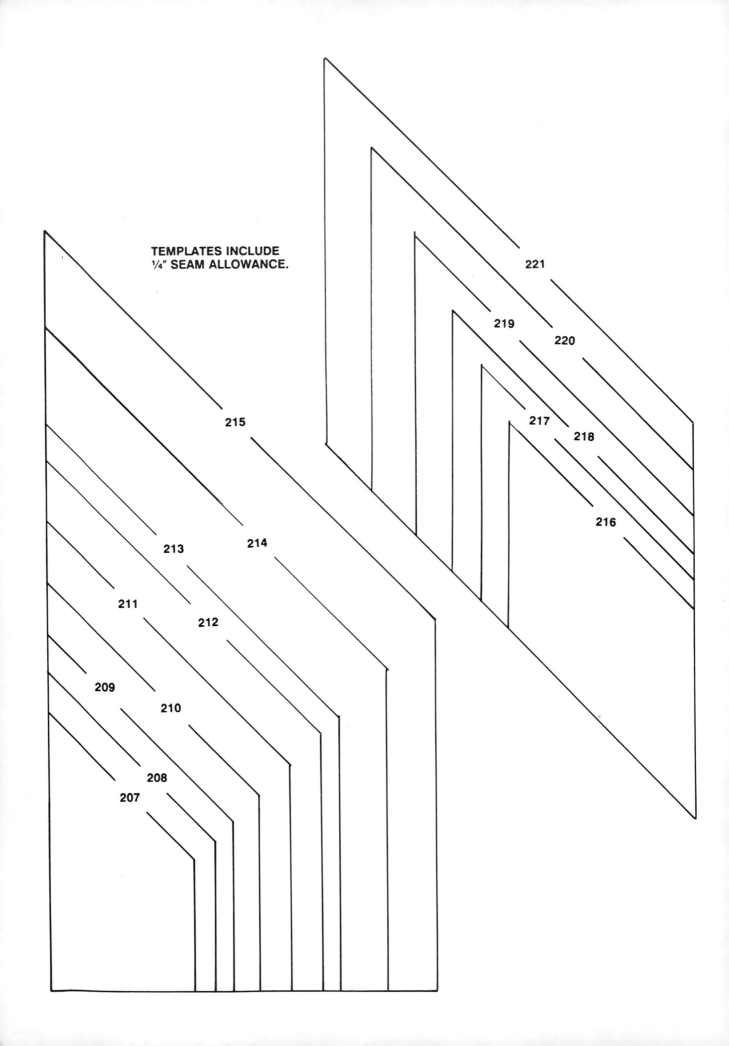

TEMPLATES INCLUDE
¼″ SEAM ALLOWANCE.

215

221

219

220

213   214

217

218

211

212

216

209

210

208

207

GLOSSARY

Backing: The fabric used on the underside of the quilt.

Baste: Temporarily secure three layers together so they can be handled while quilting, often done with long stitching.

Batting: The layer between the quilt top and the backing. Gives the quilt its "puffiness."

Bias: Diagonal to the grain.

Binding: Enclosing the fabric and batting of the outer border to create a finished edge.

Block: A quilt square made of a number of smaller pieces sewn together.

Block-by-block: Constructing a quilt by piecing and quilting each block separately. The finished blocks are then stitched together.

Borders: Fabric used around outer areas of quilt to highlight central area and enlarge the quilt to desired size.

Grain: The direction of either the horizontal or vertical threads of the fabric. Will be either parallel to the selvage or at a 90° angle to it.

Lattice: Narrow strips sewn between blocks, used to add color and to highlight the blocks.

Lattice blocks: Small squares connecting the lattice strips.

Layout: The arrangement of blocks, lattice, and borders that make up the quilt top.

Piecing: Stitching the small pieces of fabric together.

Pin-baste: Basting with safety pins. Holds more securely than thread basting. Machine foot will not catch in the basting thread.

Quilt center: The pieced quilt, before any borders are added.

Quilting: Stitching the three layers—quilt top, batting, and backing—together.

Selvage: The woven edge along the length of the fabric.

Stitch-in-the-ditch: Quilting done in a seam line.

Template: The pattern for each piece in a block.

SUPPLY LIST

Speed-Cutting Equipment

Please check your local quilt store for Miterite, Play-Plan and Speedies. If not in stock, they are available through:

Holiday Designs
507 Meadowview Lane
Coppell, Texas 75019

Check the quilt and sewing magazines for current mail-order companies. Here are some good ones:

Cabin Fever Calicoes
PO Box 550106
Atlanta, GE 30355

Clotilde
1909 SW First Ave
Ft. Lauderdale, FL 33315

Dicmar Trading Co.
PO Box 3533
Georgetown Station
Washington, DC 20007

Dover Street Booksellers
39 E. Dover St.
Easton, MD 21601

Bette Feinstein
Hard-to-Find Needlework Books
96 Roundwood Rd
Newton, MA 02164

Keepsake Quilting
PO Box 1459
Meredith, NH 03253

Nancy's Notions
PO Box 683
Beaver Dam, WI 53916

BIBLIOGRAPHY

Beyer, Jinny. *The Quilter's Album of Blocks and Borders*. EPM Publishers, 1980.

Chijiiwa, Hideaki. *Color Harmony: A Guide to Creative Color Combinations*. Greenwood Publishing, 1987.

Cody, Pat. *Continuous Line Quilting Designs: Especially for Machine Quilting*. Chilton Book Co., 1980.

Fanning, Robbie and Tony. *The Complete Book of Machine Quilting*. Chilton Book Co., 1980.

Johannah, Barbara. *Continuous Curve Quilting and The Quick Quiltmaking Handbook*. Pride of the Forest, 1980.

Khin, Yvonne M. *The Collector's Dictionary of Quilt Names and Patterns*. Acropolis Books, Ltd., 1980.

McKelvey, Susan, *Light & Shadow: Optical Illusion in Quilts*. C&T Publishing, 1989.

Total Yards

Backing | Yds

Lattice, Borders, etc. → | Block Information

Total Number | Yards

Number Per Block | Template

Swatches

Cut Sizes

Template Numbers		Lattice			Triangles		Unpieced Blocks		Borders			
		Strips	Squares		Sides	Corners			1st	2nd	3rd	4th
A												
B												
C												
D												
E												
F												
G												
H												
I												
J												
K												
L												

The Block

Play-Plan for: _____

Finished Size: _____

Block Size

Number of Pieced Blocks Needed

Backing

Building the Block

Borders and Block Layout

Notes and Photograph:

View Number and Name:

Date Started:

Date Finished:

Made By:

Made For: